M000191129

THRIVE IN THE YEAR OF THE DRAGON

Chinese Zodiac Horoscope 2024

Linda Dearsley

BENNION KEARNY

Published in 2023 by Bennion Kearny

ISBN: 978-1-915855-18-3

Linda Dearsley has asserted her right under the Copyright, Designs and Patents Act, 1988 to be identified as the author of this book.

Copyright 2023. All Rights Reserved. No part of this publication may be reproduced, stored in a retrieval system, or transmitted in any form or by any means, electronic, mechanical, photocopying, recording or otherwise, without the prior permission of the publisher.

Bennion Kearny does not have any control over, or any responsibility for, any author or third-party websites mentioned in or on this publication.

A CIP catalogue record for this book is available from the British Library.

This book is sold subject to the condition that it shall not, by way of trade or otherwise, be lent, re-sold, hired out or otherwise circulated without the publisher's prior consent in any form of binding or cover other than that it which it is published and without a similar condition including this condition being imposed on the subsequent purchaser.

TABLE OF CONTENTS

CHAPTER 1: ENTER THE DRAGON

Wow! Clear your diary, blast through those niggling chores, and free up plenty of space everywhere, because 2024 could be the year the World's been waiting for, even if it doesn't know it yet. You're not going to want to miss a thing.

On the 10th of February, the spectacular Green Wood Dragon roars into our orbit on flamboyant emerald wings, breathing fire and smoke in all directions, sending the refined Rabbit of 2023 scurrying for cover and generally upstaging every other creature in the Chinese zodiac.

The Dragon is THE mightiest of all the signs. The only mythical beast in the Chinese calendar, forever associated with royalty and the long line of Chinese Emperors (who were once believed to be descended from dragons, if not *actually* dragons themselves), the celestial Dragon is a symbol of wealth, good fortune, and ultimate power.

Multi-talented Dragon was thought to soar through the skies controlling the wind and the rain, pausing only to swoop down to the seas to sort out the planet's rivers and waterways. And should the weather turn a little chilly, a quick blast of Dragon's fiery breath could restore warmth and comfort in a trice.

So, with such a superstar in charge for the next 12 memorable months, how could 2024 not be a glittering success for all?

Time to Start Thinking Big

During the comparatively restrained year, just passed, of the elegant and refined Rabbit of 2023, most of us hopefully got a much-needed chance to slow down, reconnect with our roots, redefine our priorities and generally regroup after the roller-coaster upheavals kicked off by the revolutionary Rat of 2020 and the chaos that followed. But now we've finally got our breath back and become accustomed to the new landscape, many are longing for something a little more exciting. A little more colourful. A little more adventurous even, after all the doom and gloom.

Well, if that sounds like you, good news! Exuberant Dragon doesn't do doom and gloom. If that doesn't sound like you, sorry, but once you get used to the new vibe, you might change your mind.

The point is that Dragon thinks big. Dragon has heard of the concept: 'Small is Beautiful', plus 'Good things come in small packages', but Dragon genuinely doesn't get it. As far as Dragon is concerned, if small is beautiful, then 'Big' must be Fabulous. If good things come in small packages, just think how wonderful the contents of a really HUGE parcel, bedecked with ribbons and balloons, will be.

The Dragon likes big, bold, brightly coloured and – if possible – smothered in sequins.

'Life is Never Stagnation...'

So said one of the world's most famous Dragons and the 20th century's answer to Confucius, the great Golden Dragon himself, martial arts superstar, Bruce Lee, who was born in the Dragon year of 1940. Bruce added, '...things live by movement and gain strength as they move', which pretty much sums up the prevailing energy of 2024.

While last year's Rabbit brought us some welcome calm, too much can lead to the kind of stagnation Bruce warned about. Which is precisely why the Dragon follows so swiftly on Bunny's fluffy heels. Dragon years are renowned for incinerating stagnation and firing rip-roaring life back into the proceedings. They bring action, prosperity, progress and spectacular events to the world. They can also bring spectacular failures too, because Dragon energy is all about expansion, adventure, and taking calculated risks – and (of course) when you take a risk, things can just as easily go horribly wrong. Dragon, naturally, is quite relaxed about this and shrugs off the odd disaster as an occupational hazard.

Once again, Bruce Lee was completely in tune with his inner Dragon. 'Don't fear failure,' he once said, 'it's not failure, but low aim, that's the crime. In great attempts, it's glorious even to fail.'

Be like Bruce - Go for Glorious

In China, the Dragon is regarded as the most auspicious of the 12 signs and a Dragon year, the luckiest year of them all.

Not everyone can be born a Dragon, of course, but they can activate some of that magical Dragon luck by timing important life events to take place in a Dragon year. It's said that the birth-rate in the Chinese community soars during a Dragon year, and a baby born that year brings good fortune to the entire family. No wonder Dragon children tend to be especially cherished – everyone wants one to attract blessings to the home.

Marriages and new businesses begun in a Dragon year are believed particularly likely to flourish, and a Dragon year is also regarded as the perfect time to move into a new home, even if you won't necessarily stay there for decades. So, it seems, if you have any milestones to celebrate or ambitions to put into practise, 2024 is the year to go for gold.

The Awesome Power of Green

Dragons may be mythical creatures but nevertheless, according to tradition, they come in a range of colours. So why, you may be wondering, should we be so excited that this year's Dragon is green?

Well, according to Chinese tradition, in addition to being ruled by an animal, each year is also imbued with the energy of an element, represented by a colour. The animal ruler of the year arrives festooned in the colour of that year's element and displays the characteristics associated with the element as well as its own personality.

So Green is the colour that symbolises Wood in Chinese lore. 2024 is a Wood year. This is a bit confusing for Westerners – we tend to associate wood with the colour brown, but that's because we're thinking of different things. The Chinese Wood element represents not wood in the form of an inert plank to be nailed on a floor or turned into a piece of ̣iture. That sort of wood is just the end result of the mysterious, ̣ energy that powers a tiny seed into a mighty tree, sprouting ̣reen leaves along the way to feed the process.

̣n and growing plant life is 'Wood' as far as Chinese ̣ last leaf and tiny blade, filled with a surging, ̣ds to expand in all directions.

So, a Wood year is particularly welcome, believed as it is to unleash much-needed expansion and growth into the world. But when the Wood year rides in on the wings of the powerful, exuberant Dragon, the results are expected to be nothing short of spectacular.

Wisdom of
The Dragon

The simple act of paying attention can get you a long way.

Keanu Reeves

(1964 Wood Dragon)

Charm the Dragon

So, what will the Year of the Dragon bring to you? Will you get a share of the famous Dragon riches – that mythical hoard of priceless treasure hidden deep within the Dragon lair– or are you more likely to creep away with nothing more than a blistering blast of scorching breath and the lash of a scaley tail? How can you persuade the Dragon to swoosh some goodies in your direction?

According to Chinese astrology, it's perfectly possible to charm the Dragon if you play your cards right. Some signs get on well with the Dragon, others not so much. Yet whatever your sign, you get to choose how to respond to the Dragon year and the events that unfold. Make the kind of choices favoured by the Dragon, and the Dragon will smooth your path and offer glittering rewards. Behave in a way the Dragon dislikes and, at best, your efforts will be ignored; at worst, your plans could go up in smoke – possibly literally. You really don't want to upset the Dragon!

Yet, the secret to wooing the Dragon is deceptively simple. Once you understand the nature of the beast, how it gets on with your particular sign and why, the way ahead becomes clear. As soon as you know what you're dealing with, you can formulate a plan.

Fail to Plan, Plan to Fail

Okay, so maybe you're the go-with-the-flow type. You don't like everything nailed down; you prefer to be flexible, free to drift, following where your mood leads you. The idea of creating a strategy seems tedious. Yet, as that other legendary Golden Dragon, the iconic John Lennon, born the same year as Bruce Lee, said, 'Life is what happens while you're busy making other plans.'

What he meant was that fate has a nasty habit of intervening when we least expect it, hurling unforeseen events across the most careful of paths, throwing us off our feet or knocking us off course altogether. No matter how laid-back and spontaneous you are, you're bound to have to apply for a job now and then, organise the occasional holiday, arrange a party or a home move, take an exam – all the kinds of plans that could proceed as smoothly as a knife through butter, or spiral out of control like a runaway train if hit by a sudden bolt from the blue.

Wouldn't it be wonderful if we weren't so vulnerable? If we could know in advance what sort of challenges might be heading our way? Or when unexpected opportunities might appear, so we can seize them before they slip away?

Well, according to Chinese lore, we can.

Work Smart

Each New Year, the fresh energy bursting into the world is quite different from that of the year before. But it's not a completely unknown quantity. Understand what makes the new boss of the year tick, and you know what to expect.

You'd know that actions that brought you wealth and glory when the do-or-die Tiger was at the helm are likely to get bogged down in red tape when slow-moving, methodical Ox is in charge. Similarly, hilarious pranks and outrageous ideas could zoom you straight to the top in a naughty Monkey year, but wheel them out when subtle Snake's in the driver's seat, and you're more likely to get a cold, unnerving stare.

Special Dragons

The other thing to bear in mind is that not all Dragons are exactly the same. Like every creature in Chinese astrology, the Dragon comes in five different varieties. Think of them as breeds. Every Dragon has a basic Dragon personality, but each comes in a different hue, which adds to, or modifies, the Dragon character.

So, in 2024, we welcome the aforementioned Green Wood Dragon. In later years, we'll meet the Scarlet Fire Dragon, the Brown Earth Dragon, the Golden Metal Dragon and the Black (or sometimes Blue) Water Dragon – because every 12 years, a different Dragon takes a turn of being in charge. They're all Dragons, of course, but cousins rather than clones.

All Dragons are action-loving do-ers, obviously, but the Green Dragon is the busiest of them all. Bursting with expansive Wood energy, the dynamic Green Dragon just can't stop seeking fresh projects to nurture and breathe into life. And while some Dragons can turn disconcertingly fierce if irritated, the Green Dragon has more patience than most.

2023 was a watery year presided over by the Black Water Rabbit, and Wood always follows Water in the Chinese cycle. Don't expect things to carry on in much the same way. Water goes ahead to prepare the ground, leaving it irrigated and fertile, in perfect condition for all those green Woody things to sprout and grow – and once they get started, who knows what shape they'll take?

Well, maybe we can get a sneak preview. It's been 60 years since the last Green Dragon swooped onto the scene – more than half a century of hatching great plans from deep in its lair. So, to get an insight into what form those plans might take, we can check out what happened when the Wood Dragon's Grandpa – the great Green Dragon of 1964 – took charge.

Meet the Glam Green Dragon of 1964 – showman par excellence

No Chinese New Year celebration would be complete without the spectacle of the long, multi-coloured Dragon, animated by scores of dancers, twisting and weaving through streets around the world, driving away evil spirits and ushering in 12 months of joy and prosperity. It's a tradition that dates back two thousand years.

There's something undeniably theatrical about the Chinese Dragon. Mythical beast it might be, but with its enormous wings and fiery breath, the outrageous Dragon brings drama and action to many a fairy-tale and stage and screen production. It's hardly surprising then that the Dragon has an affinity with show business. And, as it happened, 1964 was a true glory year for the entertainment industry and its close relative, the sports world. Some say, the most exciting year of the century. Many stars and productions that shot into the limelight in 1964 have remained household names ever since.

A World Desperate for Delight

After the sombre events of 1963, when the assassination of President Kennedy rocketed a tidal wave of grief and shock from the USA right around the globe, it was as if the whole world was longing for some light relief. And so, with perfect theatrical timing, as midnight struck on the 13th of February 1964, in swirled the gorgeous Green Dragon, dominating the stage and instantly spinning a star-spangled spotlight onto the USA to extinguish the sadness.

As it happened, just a few days earlier, as the new energy was building ready for Dragon's grand entrance, the Beatles – still a fledgling British group – had flown out to America. Their manager had managed to secure them a spot on TV star Ed Sullivan's famous show on February the 9th, plus two further appearances booked (though they didn't realise it) for the auspicious early days of the Dragon year – February 16th and 23rd.

Twist and Shout

Seventy-three million viewers tuned in for that first show, and by the third, just two weeks later, something extraordinary had happened. Morose USA shook off its mourning and young people across the land were twisting and shouting with the Beatles. Blazing Dragon power had transformed four Liverpool lads into international superstars – changing the face of pop music forever.

US folk icon Bob Dylan realised it immediately. Driving with friends in California that month, he was transfixed when the Beatles record 'I Want to Hold Your Hand' suddenly burst onto the car radio. Dylan had never heard anything like it. 'Did you hear that?' he yelled to his companions. 'Man, that was f___ing' great!' 'They were doing things nobody else was doing,' he reflected later, 'Their chords were outrageous, just outrageous, but their harmonies made it all valid. Everybody thought they were just for teeny-boppers. But it was obvious to me they had staying power. I knew they were pointing the direction of where music had to go.'

Meanwhile, Dragon power was blasting the Beatles to ever greater heights. A couple of days after their second show, the Fab Four visited Miami and in the midst of a hasty schedule of promotional work, found themselves whisked to a gym for a comic photo session with an upstart young boxer who was in training for an audacious crack at the World Heavyweight Title. Aged just 22, the cheeky young chancer was a lad called Cassius Clay, the Beatles were told. A name he later changed to Muhammad Ali. Young Clay obligingly danced around the British lads, in his satin shorts and boxing-gloves, play-fighting for the cameras and the lads obligingly fell to the floor like a row of skittles. A hilarious time was had by all.

Dragon power was at work on Cassius Clay as well as the Fab Four. A week later, the boxing world was rocked when young Clay defeated the reigning champion Sonny Liston and took the World Heavyweight title for himself. Like the Beatles, he became an international legend, regarded today as the greatest boxer of the 20th century.

Wisdom of
The Dragon

Everything will be okay
in the end. If it's not okay,
it's not the end.

John Lennon
(1940 Gold Dragon)

The British Invasion

Hardly pausing to draw breath, the Beatles returned to the UK, this time to make a film – a musical in a ground-breaking documentary style, called A Hard Day's Night. The movie proved to be another triumph – after which the Fab Four went back to churning out more and more hits. By the time the Dragon roared away in early 1965, they'd scored six number-one singles in the charts.

It wasn't just the Beatles turning the music scene upside down. The Rolling Stones released their first album that April, and everywhere you looked, British bands were storming the charts. The UK couldn't contain them. The Who, the Kinks, the Small Faces, The Animals, Herman's Hermits… So many British groups were sweeping the USA, the American media began talking about 'The British Invasion'.

Can't stop the Music

Within the UK, demand for the exciting new sounds couldn't be constrained. Determined to evade the stuffy old BBC's monopoly on radio broadcasting and its meagre ration of pop music, Ronan O'Rahilly, a young Irish businessman, launched Radio Caroline (named, he said, after the assassinated President Kennedy's small daughter Caroline) on board a ship, anchored just outside British territorial waters off Felixstowe, and beyond the reach of the restrictive licensing laws. Dubbed Radio Pirates, Caroline's DJs braved storms and seasickness to play pop music all day long – to the delight of British teenagers everywhere.

So successful was the venture, other Pirate stations began broadcasting, and the most successful – Radio London – was beaming out the hits by Christmas.

Creativity in Overdrive

It wasn't just the music industry that was booming in the Dragon year. Inspiration was bursting out all over. On TV, new show after new show thrilled viewers, many of which are still familiar today. Bewitched, The Man From Uncle, The Addams Family, The Munsters, Stingray, The Likely Lads, and the trendy new soap set in a motel – Crossroads – all aired for the first time in 1964.

At the cinema, as well as the Beatles' sensational A Hard Day's Night, the new James Bond film, Goldfinger, hit the screens along with My Fair Lady starring Rex Harrison and Audrey Hepburn, the moody Western, A Fistful of Dollars, and the whimsical musical blockbuster, Mary Poppins – which went on to win five Academy Awards.

The world's authors were just as busy. That year, Roald Dahl published Charlie and the Chocolate Factory, Agatha Christie debuted her Caribbean Mystery, John le Carré introduced The Spy Who Came in from the Cold, and Ian Fleming's next James Bond novel, You Only Live Twice, arrived in March.

Champagne Corks Popping

Celebrations were fizzing everywhere. Queen Elizabeth and her husband, Prince Philip, welcomed their fourth child, Prince Edward, in March. Later the same month, scandalous movie stars Richard Burton and Elizabeth Taylor, whose affair upset even the Pope, finally divorced their former partners and married each other in a civil ceremony at the swanky Ritz Carlton Hotel in Montreal.

In July, British daredevil Donald Campbell set the world land speed record of 403.1mph at Lake Eyrie Salt Flats in Australia. In October, the world's finest athletes gathered in Tokyo for the Summer Olympics, with the USA and Russia bagging the biggest hauls of gold – 36 gold medals for the USA, 30 for Russia.

In December, Baptist minister and activist Martin Luther King, 35, became the youngest person to be awarded the Nobel Peace Prize for 'his non-violent struggle for civil rights for Afro-Americans'. And on December 31st, the irrepressible speed freak Donald Campbell was at it again, clocking up his second world record of the year by achieving 274.33 mph on water at Dumbleyung Lake, Australia. Campbell is the only person ever to have set both land and water speed records in the same year.

Optimism Rocks

Confidence was breaking out all over. In Britain, an October general election swept the ruling Conservative party from power after 13 years, and the incoming Labour Prime Minister, Harold Wilson, captured the mood of the nation with a spine-tingling speech promising a 'brand new Britain forged in a white heat of technology.'

The following month, US caretaker leader Lyndon Johnson won the Presidential election by a landslide. Underlining the feel-good factor, growth in both countries soared. In the US, it hit 6.4%; in the UK 5.5%.

There was talk of New Towns to be built in the UK, and a tunnel under the sea linking Britain with France. In the USA, President Johnson signed the Civil Rights Act, making discrimination on the basis of race, colour, religion, sex, or national origin, illegal. It was said to be the most sweeping civil rights legislation since the Civil War.

Even children were included in Dragon's innovations. GI Joe, a tough, action-man toy soldier with '21 moving parts' (absolutely never to be described as a doll), was launched, and instantly became top of every boy's Christmas list. At the same time, for girls, Barbie's cute kid sister, Skipper, joined the collectable Barbie family.

And in London, Charles Cooper, a humble, middle-aged clerk from the East End, unexpectedly found himself symbolising the expansive, generous spirit of the year. Modest Charles, who still lived at home with his old mum, was stunned to win the staggering sum of £225,000 on the football pools – equivalent to over £6 million today. Like a true, noble Dragon, Charles immediately promised £60,000 to his relatives and then sent a substantial cheque to his local council to pay the rent for every tenant on his estate – nearly 1,000 households.

Wood Turns Destructive

The great thing about Wood energy is that it encourages growth to flourish – which is usually a good thing. Yet, we tend to forget that, in the same way that trees can produce wonderful spreading canopies, reaching for the sky, their roots – burrowing deep into the ground – are capable of toppling walls and crumbling foundations. Wood can be just as destructive as it is creative. In fact, Chinese astrologers have a saying: 'Wood breaks Earth'.

And it did so with a vengeance in Alaska in 1964. Around teatime on the 27th of March that year – which happened to be Good Friday – people living around the huge bay and waterways of picturesque Prince William Sound were startled by a terrible grinding, crunching sound. Then, the earth beneath their feet began to buck and tremble and the tarmacked roads rose and undulated before their eyes, like waves on the sea.

The USA's strongest ever earthquake, measuring 9.2 in magnitude, struck Prince William Sound, southeast of Anchorage and lasted four agonising minutes, locals said.

Buildings collapsed, roads and railway tracks were torn up, parts of the coast sank eight feet, while others rose 38 feet. Coastal forests plunged below sea level and were destroyed by salt water and then the tremors triggered devastating tsunamis and landslides. One hundred and thirty-one people were killed that day, and the after-shocks continued for a year.

The disaster has been known ever since as the Great Alaska Earthquake.

Meet The Dynamic Green Dragon of 2024

So, taking account of what happened last time the Green Dragon got to direct the action, what can we expect from 2024?

Chances are we'll notice a change of pace almost immediately. As the gentle Rabbit exits discreetly over the horizon, the Dragon is unlikely to tiptoe bashfully onto the scene. Crashing cymbals, whirling strobe lights – metaphorically speaking, of course – creating an entrance you just can't miss… that's Dragon's style.

Expect big, possibly surprising announcements almost immediately. Projects that have been dragging on, going nowhere, are likely to be terminated abruptly and objections squashed. Procrastinators in every walk of life will be invited to get on with it or go. Opportunities will evaporate like morning mist in hesitant hands, to be bestowed instead on bolder recipients. There could be unexpected resignations and equally unlikely appointments.

And, all around, we could notice a general mending and smartening up of our surroundings. Shabbiness and disarray encourage stagnation, the Dragon believes, which can't be tolerated.

Wisdom of
The Dragon

We seek to last,
more than we try to live.

Andy Warhol

(1928 Earth Dragon)

All the World's a Stage

As in 1964, showbusiness and sport can expect a huge boost. The movie world is already gearing up to wow audiences in 2024 with 12 months of unmissable treats. Okay, so most of the new blockbusters are sequels – but then the Dragon dance is performed every year and never loses its lustre. Dragon's quite happy to repeat a winning formula.

We can expect Kung Fu Panda 4 (Bruce Lee would approve), Deadpool 3, Despicable Me 4, Bad Boys 4, Mission Impossible, Dead Reckoning Part 2 – the eighth instalment of the series, then there's Beetlejuice 2, Gladiator 2 and, echoing perhaps the 1964 inspiration of Mary Poppins, the film version of the musical Wicked will also make its debut.

The Dragon likes to rock, so just as in 1964, we can expect a renewed focus on the music scene. Previously little-known musicians will shoot to stardom, but the old favourites will be welcomed too. Queen, Madonna, Coldplay, Yes, Taylor Swift are just a few of the stars scheduled to tour.

And just as in 1964, 2024 is an Olympic Year and sees the flaming torch heading for Paris. The Games kick off in July and are followed by the Para-Olympics at the end of August. Since French President Macron was born a celestial Snake, a great friend of the Dragon, it looks like the Games will be a triumph.

Business Booms

Under the burgeoning Wood influence, new ventures will be sprouting everywhere. Especially-favoured will be any business that actually involves wood – furniture, carving, retro wooden boats, garden offices, flooring – but also businesses that grow things, such as plant nurseries, garden centres, forestry, farms, and orchards. All should do well. Flower shows from the iconic Chelsea downwards will enjoy a spectacular year and inspire green-fingered copycats everywhere.

But Wood energy also inspires creative endeavours of every kind, so writers, artists, gaming creators, and designers will find themselves suddenly ablaze with new ideas while Dragon power will blast them to success.

And since this year's Dragon is green by nature as well as by name, innovative eco-projects, especially *big, audacious* eco-projects, will unexpectedly get the go-ahead.

We're also likely to see some exciting scientific breakthroughs in 2024, especially in the fields of alternative energy and renewable materials.

Leadership déjà vu

Strangely enough, if Grandpa Green Dragon of 1964 arrived in our 21st-century world and checked out the political scene of 2024, he might be surprised to find nothing much had changed.

For a start, back in '64, there were two major leadership elections; in the USA and also in Britain.

And by an odd coincidence, at the time, both countries were being run by caretaker leaders.

In the USA, former Vice-President Lyndon Johnson had stepped in following the death of President Kennedy, while in Britain, Conservative Sir Alec Douglas-Home, had been hastily installed following the resignation of PM Harold Macmillan, after a scandal.

Now, as 2024 dawns, there are once again two major leadership elections due, in the USA and also in Britain.

What's more, many people believe a caretaker leader could well be running the USA before the presidential election due to the frailty of Joe Biden, while in Britain, Conservative PM Rishi Sunak was hastily installed – unelected by the voting public – following the resignations of PM Boris Johnson and his successor, after a scandal.

Back in 1964, Lyndon Johnson won the US election by a landslide, but in Britain, Sir Alec was defeated by the rival Labour party, ending 13 years of Conservative rule. Could history repeat itself? The Green Dragon reckons it will.

Over in Russia, it was all change, too. On October 14th 1964, long-running leader Nikita Khrushchev was brutally deposed by rival Leonid Brezhnev.

With Russia's current long-running President Putin facing mounting difficulties, could 2024 see the arrival of a new Russian leader, too?

Only time will tell, but in every case, Green Dragon energy will ensure the strongest, boldest candidates will win.

Wisdom of
The Dragon

Never a failure,
always a lesson.

Rihanna

(1988 Earth Dragon)

Work more Fun than Fun

The flamboyant Green Dragon may look frivolous in a scary kind of way, but that technicolour exterior hides a serious work ethic. Suddenly, everyone's buzzing to get on and make a name for themselves or at least to make a difference. This time next year, there really will be a great many more millionaires.

People who previously boasted about coasting along with very little effort will find few admirers in 2024. Talent, persistence, and sheer hard work are the sought-after qualities this year. Working hours could grow longer. Yet the Dragon loves a good time, and while the mood may be to spend more time at work, many a workplace could suddenly become more fun.

Successful employers will start encouraging staff to socialise during the working day and enjoy staff get-togethers at the end of it. Company gyms, choirs, and quiz nights could spring up. Staff competitions and awards ceremonies encouraged. Work might not truly end up becoming more fun than fun, but it's likely to get a whole lot more enjoyable.

And people who really loathe their jobs, and just can't see any way to appreciate them further, are not overlooked by the Dragon. Suddenly, the impetus to change careers or companies will present itself and they're likely to find themselves in a whole new setup by 2025.

Festivals and Festivities

We're all likely to be busy in 2024, but not too busy for the occasional break. Trips that combine work with pleasure are especially favoured, but Dragon energy also powers getaways involving the arts. Music Festivals, carnivals, pageants, open-air theatre, and cultural galas are likely to flourish, as well as opportunities to volunteer for similar events. Think historical re-enactments, archaeological digs, a visitor guide for tourist attractions, a museum assistant.

And, for longer holidays, Dragon – of course – zooms around on outstretched wings, so overseas trips by plane to warm destinations will be more popular than ever, with countries associated with dragons – such as China, Vietnam, Japan, and even Wales – becoming surprisingly alluring.

Wisdom of
The Dragon

A goal is not always meant to be reached, it often serves simply as something to aim at.

Bruce Lee

(1940, Gold Dragon)

Why is the Year called Dragon?

According to Chinese folklore, there are many explanations as to why the calendar is divided up the way it is. Perhaps the most popular is the story about the supreme Jade Emperor who lives in heaven. He decided to name each year in honour of a different animal and decreed that a race would be run to decide which animals would be chosen, and the order in which they would appear.

Twelve animals arrived to take part. Actually, in one legend there were 13, and included the cat, at the time a great friend of the rat. But the cat was a sleepy creature and asked the rat to wake him in time for the race and in the excitement (or was it by design?), the rat forgot and dashed off, leaving the cat fast asleep. The cat missed the race and missed out on getting a year dedicated to his name. Which is why cats have hated rats ever since.

Anyway, as they approached the finish line, the 12 competitors found a wide river blocking their route. The powerful Ox, a strong swimmer, plunged straight in, but the tiny Rat begged to be carried across on his back. Kindly Ox agreed, but when they reached the opposite bank, the wily Rat scampered down Ox's body, jumped off his head and shot across the finish line in first place. Which is why the Rat is the first animal of the Chinese zodiac, followed by the Ox.

The muscular Tiger, weighed down by his magnificent coat, arrived in third place, followed by the non-swimming Rabbit who'd found some rocks downstream and hopped neatly from one to another, until it spotted a log floating downstream and jumped on to be carried safely to dry land.

The Emperor was surprised to see the Dragon with his great wings, fly in, in fifth place, instead of the expected first. The Dragon explained that while high up in the sky he saw a village in flames and the people running out of their houses in great distress, so he'd made a detour and employed his rain-making skills (Chinese Dragons can create water as well as fire) to put out the blaze before returning to the race. In some versions of the story, Dragon also adds that as he approached the river he spotted poor little Rabbit clinging perilously to a log, so Dragon gently blew the log across and watched to see Rabbit safely ashore before flying over himself.

In sixth place came the Snake. Clever as the Rat, the Snake had wrapped himself around one of the Horse's hooves and hung on while the Horse swam the river. When the Horse climbed ashore, the Snake slithered off, so startling the Horse that it reared up in alarm, allowing the Snake to slide over the finish line ahead of him.

The Goat, Monkey, and Rooster arrived next at the river. They spotted some driftwood and rope washed up on the shore, so Monkey deftly lashed them together to make a raft and the three of them hopped aboard and floated across. The Goat jumped off first, swiftly followed by Monkey and Rooster. They found they'd beaten the Dog, which was unexpected as the Dog was a good swimmer.

It turned out the Dog so enjoyed the water, he'd hung around playing in the shallows emerging only in time to come eleventh. Last of all came the Pig, not the best of swimmers, and further slowed by his decision to pause for a good meal before exerting himself in the current.

And so, the wheel of the zodiac was set forevermore, with the Year of the Rat beginning the cycle, followed by the Ox, Tiger, Rabbit, Dragon, Snake, Horse, Goat, Monkey, Rooster, Dog and Pig.

How to Succeed in 2024

So, since 2024 is the Year of the Dragon, how will you fare? Does the Dragon present your astrological animal with opportunities or challenges? As the fable about how the years got their names shows, every one of the astrological animals is resourceful in its own special way. Faced with the daunting prospect of crossing the river, each successfully made it to the other side, even the creatures that could barely swim.

So, whether your year animal gets on easily with the Green Wood Dragon, or whether they have to work at their relationship, you can make 2024 a wonderful year to remember.

Chinese Astrology has been likened to a weather forecast. Once you know whether you'll need your umbrella or your suntan lotion, you can step out with confidence and enjoy the trip.

Find Your Chinese Astrology Sign

To find your Chinese sign, just look up your birth year in the table below.

Important note: if you were born in January or February, check the dates of the New Year very carefully. The Chinese New Year follows the lunar calendar and the beginning and end dates are not fixed, but vary each year. If you were born before mid-February, your animal sign might actually be the sign of the previous year. For example, 1980 was the year of the Monkey, but the Chinese New Year began on February 16, so a person born in January or early February 1980 would belong to the year before – the year of the Goat.

And there's More to it Than That...

In case you're saying to yourself, but surely, how can every person born in the same 365 days have the same personality(?) – you're quite right. The birth year is only the beginning.

Your birth year reflects the way others see you and your basic characteristics, but your month and time of birth are also ruled by the celestial animals – probably different animals from the one that dominates your birth year. The personalities of these other animals modify and add talents to those you acquired with your birth year creature.

The 1920s

5 February 1924 – 24 January 1925 | RAT

25 January 1925 – 12 February 1926 | OX

13 February 1926 – 1 February 1927 | TIGER

2 February 1927 – 22 January 1928 | RABBIT

23 January 1928 – 9 February 1929 | DRAGON

10 February 1929 – 29 January 1930 | SNAKE

The 1930s

30 January 1930 – 16 February 1931 | HORSE

17 February 1931 – 5 February 1932 | GOAT

6 February 1932 – 25 January 1933 | MONKEY

26 January 1933 – 13 February 1934 | ROOSTER

14 February 1934 – 3 February 1935 | DOG

4 February 1935 – 23 January 1936 | PIG

24 January 1936 – 10 February 1937 | RAT

11 February 1937 – 30 January 1938 | OX

31 January 1938 – 18 February 1939 | TIGER

19 February 1939 – 7 February 1940 | RABBIT

The 1940s

8 February 1940 – 26 January 1941 | DRAGON

27 January 1941 – 14 February 1942 | SNAKE

15 February 1942 – 4 February 1943 | HORSE

5 February 1943 – 24 January 1944 | GOAT

25 January 1944 – 12 February 1945 | MONKEY

13 February 1945 – 1 February 1946 | ROOSTER

2 February 1946 – 21 January 1947 | DOG

22 January 1947 – 9 February 1948 | PIG

10 February 1948 – 28 January 1949 | RAT

29 January 1949 – 16 February 1950 | OX

The 1950s

17 February 1950 – 5 February 1951 | TIGER

6 February 1951 – 26 January 1952 | RABBIT

27 January 1952 – 13 February 1953 | DRAGON

14 February 1953 – 2 February 1954 | SNAKE

3 February 1954 – 23 January 1955 | HORSE

24 January 1955 – 11 February 1956 | GOAT

12 February 1956 – 30 January 1957 | MONKEY

31 January 1957 – 17 February 1958 | ROOSTER

18 February 1958 – 7 February 1959 | DOG

8 February 1959 – 27 January 1960 | PIG

The 1960s

28 January 1960 – 14 February 1961 | RAT

15 February 1961 – 4 February 1962 | OX

5 February 1962 – 24 January 1963 | TIGER

25 January 1963 – 12 February 1964 | RABBIT

13 February 1964 – 1 February 1965 | DRAGON

2 February 1965 – 20 January 1966 | SNAKE

21 January 1966 – 8 February 1967 | HORSE

9 February 1967 – 29 January 1968 | GOAT

30 January 1968 – 16 February 1969 | MONKEY

17 February 1969 – 5 February 1970 | ROOSTER

The 1970s

6 February 1970 – 26 January 1971 | DOG

27 January 1971 – 14 February 1972 | PIG

15 February 1972 – 2 February 1973 | RAT

3 February 1973 – 22 January 1974 | OX

23 January 1974 – 10 February 1975 | TIGER

11 February 1975 – 30 January 1976 | RABBIT

31 January 1976 – 17 February 1977 | DRAGON

18 February 1977 – 6 February 1978 | SNAKE

7 February 1978 – 27 January 1979 | HORSE

28 January 1979 – 15 February 1980 | GOAT

The 1980s

16 February 1980 – 4 February 1981 | MONKEY

5 February 1981 – 24 January 1982 | ROOSTER

25 January 1982 – 12 February 1983 | DOG

13 February 1983 – 1 February 1984 | PIG

2 February 1984 – 19 February 1985 | RAT

20 February 1985 – 8 February 1986 | OX

9 February 1986 – 28 January 1987 | TIGER

29 January 1987 – 16 February 1988 | RABBIT

17 February 1988 – 5 February 1989 | DRAGON

6 February 1989 – 26 January 1990 | SNAKE

The 1990s

27 January 1990 – 14 February 1991 | HORSE

15 February 1991 – 3 February 1992 | GOAT

4 February 1992 – 22 January 1993 | MONKEY

23 January 1993 – 9 February 1994 | ROOSTER

10 February 1994 – 30 January 1995 | DOG

31 January 1995 – 18 February 1996 | PIG

19 February 1996 – 7 February 1997 | RAT

8 February 1997 – 27 January 1998 | OX

28 January 1998 – 5 February 1999 | TIGER

6 February 1999 – 4 February 2000 | RABBIT

The 2000s

5 February 2000 – 23 January 2001 | DRAGON

24 January 2001 – 11 February 2002 | SNAKE

12 February 2002 – 31 January 2003 | HORSE

1 February 2003 – 21 January 2004 | GOAT

22 January 2004 – 8 February 2005 | MONKEY

9 February 2005 – 28 January 2006 | ROOSTER

29 January 2006 – 17 February 2007 | DOG

18 February 2007 – 6 February 2008 | PIG

7 February 2008 – 25 January 2009 | RAT

26 January 2009 – 13 February 2010 | OX

The 2010s

14 February 2010 – 2 February 2011 | TIGER

3 February 2011 – 22 January 2012 | RABBIT

23 January 2012 – 9 February 2013 | DRAGON

10 February 2013 – 30 January 2014 | SNAKE

31 January 2014 – 18 February 2015 | HORSE

19 February 2015 – 7 February 2016 | GOAT

8 February 2016 – 27 January 2017 | MONKEY

28 January 2017 – 15 February 2018 | ROOSTER

16 February 2018 – 4 February 2019 | DOG

5 February 2019 – 24 January 2020 | PIG

The 2020s

25 January 2020 – 11 February 2021 | RAT

12 February 2021 – 31 January 2022 | OX

1 February 2022 – 21 January 2023 | TIGER

22 January 2023 – 9 February 2024 | RABBIT

10 February 2024 – 28 January 2025 | DRAGON

29 January 2025 – 16 February 2026 | SNAKE

17 February 2026 – 5 February 2027 | HORSE

6 February 2027 – 25 January 2028 | GOAT

26 January 2028 – 12 February 2029 | MONKEY

13 February 2029 – 2 February 2030 | ROOSTER

CHAPTER 2: THE DRAGON

Dragon Years

23 January 1928 – 9 February 1929

8 February 1940 – 26 January 1941

27 January 1952 – 13 February 1953

13 February 1964 – 1 February 1965

31 January 1976 – 17 February 1977

17 February 1988 – 5 February 1989

5 February 2000 – 23 January 2001

23 January 2012 – 9 February 2013

10 February 2024 – 28 January 2025

28 January 2036 – 14 February 2037

Natural Element: Wood

Will 2024 be a Golden Year for the Dragon?

Okay, Dragon, this is it. You might like to clear any furniture out of the way and warn bystanders to stand well back – because this is a momentous occasion. After 12 long, sometimes excruciating years, your time has come.

At last, you can unfold those vast, shimmering wings, shake them loose, stretch them wide – wider still – and then soar up and up, high as you like, into that blue, blue sky.

2024 is yours! You are officially the ruler of the year. The whole world is spread out at your feet. All you've got to do now, Dragon, is decide what you're going to do with it!

To be fair, if you're typical of your sign, 2023 wasn't too bad for Dragons. Not like some previous years we could mention that you'd probably prefer to forget right now. The great thing about you and the gentle Rabbit of 2023 is that although you're not exactly besties – you respect each other (from a safe distance on Rabbit's part) – and you help each other out when required.

So, many a Dragon found themselves bouncing along reasonably well in 2023. There may not have been any spectacular achievements, but there weren't any dramatic disasters either.

You may not have added appreciably to that Dragon hoard, but many Dragons have reconnected with old friends and long-lost family members as well as rediscovering a social life. Remember social life, Dragon? These are precious treasures the Black Water Rabbit brought you.

Chances are, though, you won't realise quite how much the Black Rabbit did for you until 2024 unfolds a little more.

This is because the Dragon is a Wood creature, and this is a Wood year. The Black Water Rabbit has left you fertile ground, well irrigated, and in perfect condition for all your projects to burst into life.

Last year, even if you didn't immediately recognise them, Dragons received the keys to all kinds of opportunities, courtesy of the Black Rabbit. They may not have looked much back then, but just wait to see what amazing doors they open in 2024.

Suddenly, everyone wants a Dragon to work with them, spend time with them, and inspire them. Dragon suggestions that were once dismissed as impractical, unaffordable, or just too plain whacky are welcomed as strokes of genius in 2024.

All that positive energy has an amazing effect on your creativity, Dragon. Your mind's whirling like a Catherine Wheel, shooting brilliant ideas like sparks of fire in all directions.

Your natural Wood energy always aims for growth and expansion, but coupled with the vitality of a Wood year the way it is in 2024, you're so hyper your current setup is just not big enough to contain you.

Promotion beckons for employed Dragons, while self-employed and business Dragons will be deluged with work. Yet the success doesn't end there; it's still not enough. Many Dragons will be inspired to add to their efforts: side hustles, second jobs, new ventures, freelance schemes. Suddenly, you've got the energy and opportunity to explore them all.

Who said you can't do two things at once? Why not make it 12? That's Dragon philosophy this year.

Not all will work out, of course, but stick with the most exciting and huge success is likely to be yours, Dragon. Wealth will follow and – at last – your bank account will reflect your true worth and talents, though if you're typical of your sign, you're not really motivated by money. Cash is always welcome, naturally, but what the real Dragon wants is excitement, a mission, and the chance to make things happen. All of these are on offer in 2024, and by 2025, you could see your name in lights.

Yet, while work projects blossom all around, many Dragons will have energy left over to expand other areas of their lives. A new, larger home beckons for some, while others will take on a second. Country Dragons suddenly fancy a pad in town, while town Dragons, a retreat in the country. Whether you end up in a caravan or a castle, you'll find a way of having the best of both worlds, Dragon.

Then there are new friends, new romance, new hobbies, and maybe even a new baby Dragon in the family – in fact, 2024 will be packed so full of excitement, chances are you'll still be talking about it long after 2025 has ended.

What it Means to Be a Dragon

To be honest, Dragon, it's not really fair. Your sign has so many advantages. When you're on good form, your personality is so dazzling the other signs need sunglasses.

The only mythical creature in the celestial cycle, the Dragon is regarded as the most fortunate of signs, and every couple hopes for a Dragon baby. To this day, the birth rate tends to rise by about 5% in the Chinese community in Dragon years.

Dragons are usually strong, healthy, and blessed with enormous self-confidence and optimism. Even if they're not conventionally good-looking, they stand out in a crowd. They're charismatic, with magnetic personalities, formidable energy, and people look up to them. Dragons are so accustomed to attention that they rarely question why this should be the case. It just seems like the natural way of the world.

These people think BIG. They're visionaries, bubbling with original new ideas, and their enthusiasm is so infectious, their optimism so strong, they easily inspire others. Without even trying, Dragons are born leaders and happily sweep their teams of followers into whatever new venture they've just dreamed up.

The only downside to this is that Dragons are easily bored. Trivial matters – such as details – irritate them, and they're keen to rush on to the next challenge before they've quite finished the first.

With a good second in command, who can attend to the picky minutiae, all could be well. If not, Dragon's schemes can go spectacularly wrong. Yet, it hardly seems to matter. The Dragon subscribes to the theory that you have to fail your way to success. Setbacks are quickly forgotten as Dragon launches excitedly into the next adventure, and quite often – given the Dragon's good luck – this works.

People born under this sign often receive success and wealth, yet they are not materialistic. They're generous and kind in an absent-minded way, and care far more about having a worthy goal than any rewards it might bring. And it is vital for the Dragon to have a goal. A Dragon without a goal is a sad, dispirited creature – restless and grumpy.

Even if it's not large, the Dragon home gives the impression of space and light. Dragons hate to feel confined in any way. They like to look out the window and see lots of sky and have clear, uncluttered surfaces around them, even if it's difficult for Dragons to keep them that way.

Yet the Dragon home could have a curiously un-lived-in feel. This is because the Dragon regards home as a lair – a comfortable base from which to plan the next project rather than a place to spend a lot of time.

Dragons love to travel, but they don't really mind where they go as long as it's different and interesting. Yet, despite so much going for them, Dragons often feel misunderstood. Their impatience with trivia extends to the irritating need for tact and diplomacy at times. Dragon doesn't get this. If Dragon has something to say, they say it. Why waste time dressing it up in fancy words, they think? But then people get upset, and Dragon is baffled. It's not always easy being a Dragon.

Best Jobs for Dragon 2024

The Boss

President

Journalist

Film Director

Professor

Motivational Speaker

Architect

Lecturer

Perfect Partners

Cupid's arrow can strike anywhere at any time, of course, but once the novelty of new romance wears off, some relationships are easier to maintain than others. Here's a guide to the Dragon's compatibility with other signs.

Dragon with Dragon

When Dragon meets Dragon, onlookers tend to take a step back and hold their breath. These two are a combustible mix – they either love each other or loathe each other. They are so alike it could go either way. Both dazzling in their own orbits, they can't fail to notice the other's charms, but since they both need to be centre stage, things could get competitive. With give and take and understanding this match could work well, but it won't be easy.

Dragon with Snake

Surprisingly, this couple gets along beautifully. Snake's elegant appearance and quick but subtle mind intrigues Dragon, while Snake admires Dragon's success and endless energy. Snake has no need to battle for the limelight and is quite happy to sit back and support Dragon's schemes from the comfort of a stylish sofa. Which is all the encouragement Dragon needs.

Dragon with Horse

The athletic Horse is pretty good at keeping up with dashing Dragon. And Dragon appreciates a partner who enjoys getting out and about as much as Dragon does. Yet Horse might grow weary of Dragon's constant new projects and resent having to be involved. Horse likes to go off and do Horsey things at frequent intervals which Dragon tends to view as disloyal. This relationship could get fiery.

Dragon with Goat

Goat tends to baffle the busy Dragon. Dragon can see Goat is the creative type but can't understand why Goat doesn't appear to be working very hard when so much could be achieved. In fact, if they stayed together long enough, Dragon could help Goat make the most of many talents, but it's unlikely either of them can sustain enough interest for this to happen.

Dragon with Monkey

These two are likely to hit it off immediately. Each is attracted to the other's intelligence and lively presence, and Dragon's exuberance doesn't overwhelm hyperactive Monkey. What's more, though they both enjoy being surrounded by a crowd, Monkey only wants to make people laugh while Dragon hopes to inspire them to a cause. There is no conflict, so this couple can help each other to go far.

Dragon with Rooster

A Dragon and Rooster pairing will always attract attention. These two are both gorgeous beings and love to be surrounded by admirers. They will probably enjoy going out together and being seen as a couple, but in the long-term, they may not be able to provide the kind of support each secretly needs.

Entertaining for a while but probably not a lasting relationship.

Dragon with Dog

Not the easiest of combinations. Down-to-earth Dog can't see what all the fuss is about when it comes to Dragons. Unimpressed by glamour and irritated by what seems to Dog the gullibility of Dragon admirers, Dog can't be bothered to find out more. Dragon meanwhile is hurt by Dog's lack of interest. Great determination would be needed to make this work.

Dragon with Pig

While Dragon and Pig might seem to be opposites, the two of them can create a surprisingly contented relationship. Pig is quite happy for Dragon to fly around doing exciting things as long as Pig is not expected to do much more than admire profusely. Dragon appreciates Pig's uncritical support and makes allowances for Pig's lack of stamina. This couple could live in harmony.

Dragon with Rat

This couple is usually regarded as a very good match. They have much in common being action-loving, excitement-seeking personalities who hate to be bored. It takes a lot to dazzle Rat, but the Dragon's glamorous aura proves irresistible, while Dragon loves to be admired, so each enjoys being with the other. There could be the odd power struggle as these two are both strong characters but the magnetism is so intense they usually kiss and make up.

Dragon with Ox

Chalk and cheese though this pair may appear to be, there's a certain fascination between them. Ox may not approve of Dragon's showy manner but recognises Dragon's good intentions, while Dragon admires Ox's strength of character and gift for completing tasks. If each could find a way to tolerate the other's wildly different lifestyles, they might be good for each other but, long-term, Dragon's hectic pace might wear down even the Ox's legendary stamina.

Dragon with Tiger

The two biggest personalities in the zodiac would seem bound to clash. After all, these larger-than-life characters share so many similarities there's a danger they'd compete. Yet a relationship between the Tiger and Dragon often works well. They understand each other's impulsive natures, but they're also different enough to supply the support the other needs. They'd make a formidable power couple.

Dragon with Rabbit

Dragon is such a larger-than-life character, Rabbit could feel overwhelmed at times. Also, the Dragon can be rather noisy and over-dramatic, which would get on Rabbit's nerves. Yet they each admire the other's good points. If they could live next door to each other instead of under the same roof, a long-term relationship might work.

Dragon Love 2024 Style

No matter what you do this year, Dragon, you can't help but get yourself noticed. Try to sneak out in an old bin-liner with unwashed hair and filthy trainers (not that you ever would, of course), and some star-struck admirer will spot you and think you look awesome.

You just don't even have to try this year, Dragon. Your star quality could power the National Grid. Single Dragons looking for love will have so much choice it gets embarrassing. Talk about the Wood element bringing expansion. Just make sure you keep a note of who you're meeting when, and don't get dates mixed up.

Despite this, the typical Dragon is a loyal creature, and while you enjoy nothing more than basking in admiration, you're more than happy to wave farewell to your many fans at the end of the evening and go home with a special partner.

Attached Dragons – and quite a few Dragons settled down last year – may need to timetable extra slots for couple time. You're so busy and so in demand in 2024 that your partner could feel left out. On the other hand, the two of you could enjoy a blissful time organising that new home, hunting for a holiday retreat, or considering a baby Dragon.

Secrets of Success in 2024

Sooner or later, success is more or less guaranteed this year, Dragon – unless, that is, you get overconfident and mess up and squander your amazing opportunities.

How could you mess up with so much luck on your side, you might think? Frighteningly easily, it seems.

For a start, you're so brimming with confidence and energy you may well overestimate how much you can take on. Your output is phenomenal in 2024, Dragon, but even you have your limits. The trouble is you may not recognise them. Take some time to slow down, meditate even, and calmly work out in practical terms just how you're going to fit everything in.

In addition, listen to a sensible, trusted person. If they're worried you're overdoing it and might burn out, don't scoff and lash that angry tail. Recognise they have your best interests at heart and could be right. When they're concerned, it won't do any harm to take a break and relax.

Then there's your legendary impatience with details. The big picture is top priority, of course, but the details bring it into focus. Ignore the details and the big picture could crumble away before it's even fully formed. If you can't be bothered with the fiddly stuff, team up with someone who loves it.

Get all that sorted, and next stop's the stratosphere!

The Dragon Year at a Glance

January – The Rabbit Year is slowing all around you; you can feel it. But while others want to hibernate, your energy's rising.

February – Crack open the champagne. Dragon Year's arrived. Party time. Don't be too extravagant on the festivities.

March – The Dragon pad still needs clearing, but an intriguing offer beckons. You're too busy for housework.

April – Big news in the workplace. A Dragon is required to smooth the wheels and get things going.

May – A helpful person wants to assist with something exciting. Don't turn them away. They could be immensely useful in the coming months.

June – A friend encourages you to join the gym. No time, of course, but you check out exercise possibilities.

July – Work takes an artistic turn. You surprise yourself with undiscovered talents.

August – An intriguing business idea comes your way. Should you explore it further?

September – An unexpected late holiday comes your way. It would be rude to turn it down.

October – Work is going well until an irritating detail comes back to bite you. Don't get mad; get help.

November – You've met a fun new crowd. You haven't got much time but don't want to miss out. Reschedule some tasks.

December – Christmas shopping time already, but who cares? Your bank balance looks wonderful. Don't overdo it, but you can afford to be generous.

Lucky colours for 2024: Emerald Green, Silver, White

Lucky numbers for 2024: 11, 6, 7

Three Takeaways

Reach for the stars.

Listen twice as much as you speak.

Enthusiasm is wonderful but can overwhelm.
Tread carefully.

CHAPTER 3: THE SNAKE

Snake Years

10 February 1929 – 29 January 1930

27 January 1941 – 14 February 1942

14 February 1953 – 2 February 1954

2 February 1965 – 20 January 1966

18 February 1977 – 6 February 1978

6 February 1989 – 26 January 1990

24 January 2001 – 11 February 2002

10 February 2013 – 30 January 2014

29 January 2025 – 16 February 2026

15 February 2037 – 03 February 2038

Natural Element: Fire

Will 2024 be a Golden Year for the Snake?

So, can you cope with more good news, Snake? Thought so! After a pretty fair year in 2023, courtesy of the Black Rabbit, you can look forward to an even better 2024, thanks to your very good friend, the Green Dragon.

Last year, the elegant, discreet Rabbit assisted you as you did your best to de-stress and rebuild your stamina after the tumultuous year of the Tiger in 2022. Many Snakes still shudder as they recall how they were obliged to rush and race and generally whip themselves into a frantic frenzy to cope with the Tiger's furious pace. No wonder you greeted the arrival of the calm Rabbit with such relief.

Hopefully, you start 2024 feeling refreshed and re-invigorated because the Dragon – while being a great friend – is still a little overwhelming for the sinuous Snake.

The great thing for all Snakes is that the Snake is a Fire sign while the Dragon is a Wood creature and this is also a Wood year. Although, occasionally, such a combination can be uneasy since Wood is understandably a little nervous around Fire – it's also good news for the fiery Snake because Wood feeds Fire. And the more Wood on offer, the brighter and longer Fire will burn.

So, with a friendly Wood creature running the year, the Snake will never go hungry, and when that creature is as powerful as the Dragon, Snake can expect a banquet almost every day of the week!

In 2024, the Dragon will be wafting a steady stream of opportunities – some of them quite unusual – Snake's way, along with a shower of cash. There will probably be more opportunities than Snake can deal with, and in other years, this could end up feeling exhausting and difficult for Snakes. Not in 2024, though. Since they're such good chums, Dragon understands that the Snake can only manage so much, and is not offended if Snake fails to accept every career prospect.

This means you can relax, Snake, and pick and choose which offers you take on. You won't need to worry about money either because the Dragon will ensure you always have what you need.

Generous Dragon is also keen for you to expand in the areas that mean the most to you – particularly your home. Snakes currently living in smaller quarters than they'd prefer will suddenly be inspired to upgrade. It might not seem feasible as the year begins, but before 2024 closes, many a Snake will find a bigger property becomes unexpectedly available and that Snake coffers can, even more unexpectedly, cover the cost.

Before 2025 arrives, many Snakes will be basking in more luxurious surroundings and spending delightful hours redesigning and redecorating their new home.

If you're typical of your sign, you're probably not too bothered about endless travel, but 2024 could bring more trips than usual, and you may well find yourself embarking on several long journeys.

Expansive Dragon encourages adventure and discovery, and with all that Wood fuelling your energy, you suddenly find your Serpent 'get-up-and-go' carries you further and lasts much longer than ever before. Expect several exotic trips to the kind of warm, sunny locations you love. What's more, that lovely new home that's caught your eye? It could be overseas.

What it Means to Be a Snake

Imagine, for a moment, a creature that was incredibly beautiful, wise, intelligent, graceful, sophisticated and respected. A creature always unhurried, yet attaining its goals, apparently without effort.

What would you call this amazing beast? Well, if you were Chinese, you'd probably call it a Snake. That's right – a Snake.

Here, in the West, Snakes are almost as unwelcome as Rats and have been ever since Eve was persuaded to eat that apple in the Garden of Eden by a wily serpent. Most of us wouldn't have a good word to say for Snakes. Yet, in the East, it's a different story. There, all manner of positive qualities are discerned in the Snake, and the zodiac Snake is a good sign to be born under.

What's more, if we can forget all preconceived notions and look afresh at the much-maligned serpent, we have to admit there's something quite remarkable – almost magical – about the Snake.

For a start, Snakes don't have eyelids, which makes their stare particularly disconcerting. Astonishingly, they can shed their entire skins without ill effect, and slide away with a brand new, rejuvenated, wrinkle-free body – a feat many a human would envy.

Then there's the way they slither along without the need for legs – a bit repellent to a lot of people, but it can't be denied there's something uncanny about it. It's a surprisingly efficient means of locomotion too, and at times Snakes can move with astonishing speed. Quite a few of them can do this in water as well as on land, which makes them remarkably adaptable.

Snakes are in no way cuddly, but it seems even in the West we've retained a faint memory of a time when we recognised wisdom in the serpent. The Rod of Asclepius – the familiar symbol of a snake twisted around a pole – is still a widely used and recognised medical sign, seen outside pharmacies and doctors' surgeries, even if we don't know that Asclepius was the Greek God associated with healing. And in Greece, in the dim and distant past, snakes were sacred and believed to aid the sick.

The Chinese zodiac Snake is regarded as possibly the most beautiful of all the creatures, and people born under this sign somehow manage to present themselves in such an artful way, they give the illusion of beauty, even if not naturally endowed.

The Snake is physically graceful too. Each movement flowing into the next with effortless, elegant economy. Even when they're in a hurry, Snakes appear calm and unrushed, and should they arrive late for an appointment they're so charming and plausible with their excuses they're always forgiven.

This is a sign of great intelligence and subtlety. Snakes are never pushy, yet can usually slide into the heart of any situation they choose. Their clever conversation and easy charm makes them popular at any gathering. Yet, the Snake is picky. Snakes prefer to conserve their energy and don't waste it on activities and people of no interest to them. They are self-contained, quite happy with their own company if necessary, and seldom bored.

At work, Snakes are quietly ambitious, but in line with their policy of conserving energy wherever possible, they will aim for the quickest, easiest route to their goals. Just as the mythical Snake crossed the celestial river wrapped around the hoof of the Horse, the Snake is quite content to link their fortunes to those of a rising star so that Snake is carried to the top in their wake. Ever practical, the Snake has no need for an ego massage – the end result is what matters.

Other signs often mistake Snake's economy of action for laziness, but this is short-sighted. In fact, the Snake is so efficient and so clever that tasks are completed with great speed, leaving Snake with plenty of time to relax afterwards. What's more, in the same way that a Snake can shed its skin, people born under this sign are quite capable of suddenly walking out of a situation or way of life that no longer suits them, and reinventing themselves elsewhere without regret.

They tend to do this without warning, leaving their previous companions stunned. Only afterwards do people learn that the Snake has been inert and silently brooding for months. But it's no good imploring Snake to return. Snake's actions are swift and irrevocable.

The Snake home is a lovely place. Snakes have perfect taste. They like art, design, good lighting, and comfort. They're excellent hosts. They may not often entertain, unless they can delegate the chores, but when they do, they make it a stylish occasion to remember.

Snakes are known for their love of basking in the sun, and zodiac Snakes are no exception. Trips involving long hikes uphill in the pouring rain will not impress the Snake, but a smart sun-lounger by an infinity pool in a tropical paradise… well, that would be Snake's idea of heaven.

Best Jobs for Snake

Therapist

Beautician

Doctor

Clairvoyant

Designer

Political Advisor

Perfect Partners

Cupid's arrow can strike anywhere at any time, of course, but once the novelty of new romance wears off, some relationships are easier to maintain than others. Here's a guide to the Snake's compatibility with other signs.

Snake with Snake

This fine-looking couple turn heads wherever they go. Beautiful and perfectly dressed these two look like the perfect match. They never stop talking and enjoy the same interests so this could be a successful relationship. Long-term, however, there could be friction. They're both experts at getting what they want using the same sophisticated techniques, so they can see through each other.

Snake with Horse

At some level, perhaps, Horse remembers how Snake beat him in the calendar race, so despite an initial attraction, these two could be wary of each other. Snake is impressed by Horse's energy and athleticism while Horse admires Snake's elegance and charm. Yet they don't really have much in common. Deep thinking Snake could find Horse rather shallow and Horse may see Snake as frustratingly enigmatic.

Snake with Goat

Snake and Goat could enjoy many happy hours touring art galleries and exhibitions together. Neither of them craves excitement and harsh, adrenaline-boosting activities, and both appreciate creative artistic personalities. There's no pressure to compete with each other so these two would sail along quite contentedly. Not a passionate alliance but they could be happy.

Snake with Monkey

These two clever creatures ought to admire each other if only for their fine minds and, at first, it's possible they might. But unless they're really determined to make it work, it won't be long before active Monkey finds

Snake's energy-saving ways irritating, while Snake loses patience with Monkey's endless jokes.

Snake with Rooster

Surprisingly, Snake and Rooster work well together. Both gorgeous in different ways, they complement each other without competing. Snake's keen eyes can see beneath Rooster's proud facade to the sensitive, unsure person inside, while Rooster appreciates Snake's unobtrusive strength and wise words of encouragement at just the right moment. These two could be inseparable.

Snake with Dog

Some snakes seem to have an almost hypnotic power and, for some reason, Dog is particularly susceptible to these skills. We've heard of snake-charmers, but snakes can be dog-charmers and, without even trying, Snakes can find themselves the recipients of Dog devotion. Since the Dog is strong, loyal, and can be fun, Snake is not averse to this but might, in the end, find it boring.

Snake with Pig

Pig and Snake don't have a lot to say to each other. Snake can't be bothered with Pig's endless shopping, and Pig is hurt by Snake's snobbish attitude. They both enjoy the good things in life so a luxury fling could briefly be fun – a shared spa break might be a good idea – but in the long-term, this relationship is probably not worth pursuing.

Snake with Rat

The Snake shares Rat's good taste and being elegant, sophisticated, and smart will delight Rat at first sight. These two get on very well on an intellectual level but perhaps are better as good friends rather than long-term partners. The Snake's love of basking in the sun for hours strikes Rat as lazy and dull, while Rat's need to rush around doing deals and meeting people seems pointless and wearying to Snake.

Snake with Ox

Like Ox, the Snake is quietly ambitious and not given to racing around unless it's absolutely necessary. Ox, on the other hand, respects Snake's clever brain and understated elegance. These two could quickly discover how beneficial an alliance between them would be. They're both happy to give the other space when required but also step in with support when needed. This could be a very successful match.

Snake with Tiger

Not the best of romances. These two are so fundamentally different that any initial attraction is unlikely to last. Snake likes to bask and soak up the sun while Tiger wants to explore and discover. Tiger takes in the big picture at a glance and is off to the next challenge while Snake likes to pause, delve beneath the surface, and consider matters. It wouldn't take long before these two annoy each other.

Snake with Rabbit

This subtle pair could make a good combination. They both understand the value of working behind the scenes and neither has any desire to wear themselves out on endless adventures. They share a love of art, fine things, and quiet pleasures and they both enjoy an orderly home. These two could settle down very happily together.

Snake with Dragon

Surprisingly, this couple gets along beautifully. Snake's elegant appearance and quick but subtle mind intrigues Dragon, while Snake admires Dragon's success and endless energy. Snake has no need to battle for the limelight and is quite happy to sit back and support Dragon's schemes from the comfort of a stylish sofa. Zoom

Which is all the encouragement Dragon needs.

Snake Love 2024 Style

The sexy Snake has always had a mysterious, hypnotic quality – some strange power that draws partners helplessly to their sides with little more than the flicker of an eye. Well, this year, Snake magic is in overdrive.

All that Wood energy has lit your fires in a big way, Snake, and smitten admirers are falling at your feet wherever you go. You continue to be choosy, of course – you do have high standards, after all – but let's face it, there's plenty of choice. All in all, things are set to get pretty steamy around Single Snakes in 2024; in fact, there won't be much time left over to keep that career bowling along.

Attached Snakes can become quite demanding of their partners for the same reason. They want plenty of attention and appreciation. Should the partner fail to provide this, Snake is quite capable of transferring their affections to someone who can. 2024 could be a make-or-break year for many Snake relationships.

Secrets of Success in 2024

Slogging away at some strenuous job has never been the Snake route to success and events in 2024 are not going to change that. You believe in working smart, Snake, exerting no more effort than is absolutely necessary.

This approach suits your constitution very well, and you've certainly got the brainpower to achieve your goals. You've also got the Dragon on your side this year, sending you all the help you could wish for.

Yet, it's possible to have too much of a good thing. Your challenge in 2024 is to resist the temptation to grab every delectable offer that comes your way. You know you need to pace yourself and normally you can, but discipline could be more difficult this year with so much going for you and the enthusiastic Dragon urging you on. Keep a cool head and be very careful what you accept.

Then there's your love life. With your heart ruling your head, you might let success slip through your fingers if you allow yourself to get too distracted.

And, finally, you're more fiery than ever this year, which could result in a temper tantrum or two. This will astonish and possibly alarm colleagues who regard you as the quiet, sensible type. When you feel the flames rising, take a deep breath and walk away.

Snake Year at a Glance

January – You can feel the momentum building, Snake. Change is in the air. Get some rest.

February – A friendly face at work makes you smile. Things are looking up.

March – A big shopping trip looms large. You're rocking a new look, and it's going down a storm.

April – The boss has noticed you and seems to like what you're doing. Promotion? Pay rise? Everything's possible.

May – Two offers land on your desk. Must you choose, or can you accept both? Decisions, decisions.

June – The workload is piling up, but a sympathetic friend comes to your rescue.

July – A party invitation or celebration leads to romance. Watch out for jealous eyes.

August – Overspending on an expensive holiday could cause arguments. You'll get away with it, though.

September – Time to say goodbye to a tiresome face or situation. No regrets.

October – A new love wants attention. You're pretty busy, but maybe you can reschedule.

November – Celebrations at work. Whether you're welcoming a new team member or toasting a victory, make the most of it.

December – You're all set for a romantic Christmas with a special someone. Watch out for an unexpected gift.

Lucky colours for 2024: Emerald, Scarlet, Terracotta

Lucky numbers for 2024: 5, 4, 8

Three Takeaways
Think boldly.
Pace yourself.
Soak up the sunshine.

CHAPTER 4: THE HORSE

Horse Years

30 January 1930 – 16 February 1931

15 February 1942 – 4 February 1943

3 February 1954 – 23 January 1955

21 January 1966 – 8 February 1967

7 February 1978 – 27 January 1979

27 January 1990 – 14 February 1991

12 February 2002 – 31 January 2003

31 January 2014 – 18 February 2015

17 February 2026 – 5 February 2027

4 February 2038 – 23 January 2039

Natural Element: Fire

Will 2024 be a Golden Year for the Horse?

Well, Horse, it's time to groom your mane to its gleaming best, polish up those shiny shoes and generally burnish your appearance to its full magnificence because – in 2024 – you're going places.

The last few years have been pretty good for you, Horse, if you're typical of your sign. Okay, not perfect – no year ever is, but you've really been one of the favoured signs in recent times. And once again, in 2024, it looks as if you'll be lucky.

True, you and the Dragon are not such good mates as you and your stripy friend the Tiger, so things won't flow as smoothly as they did when Tiger was in charge back in 2022. Nevertheless, the Dragon admires your strong physique, good looks, and feisty nature and is quite happy to help you achieve your horsey goals.

On top of that, this is a Wood year, the Dragon is a Wood creature and your natural Horse element is Fire. This combination can be both encouraging but also tricky.

Tricky because, for obvious reasons, Wood can be nervous around Fire, and since you're not complete besties, the Dragon is a little wary of you, Horse. This wariness could manifest in Dragon's bountiful opportunities taking a little longer to arrive than seems reasonable, or alternatively, the opportunities arrive but turn out to be quite a distance from your usual homestead.

Encouraging, though, because since Wood feeds hungry Fire, you've got the best part of the deal. All year, that blast of invigorating energy will propel you on to achieve more than you ever thought possible.

Your finest prospects, Horse, will be far from home. Job offers, business plans, creative ventures – all will come your way as long as you go out and about to attract their attention.

Mouth-watering career prospects beckon, but the best of them require you to commute, travel regularly or relocate altogether.

Many Horses will be house-hunting to set up home nearer their job, while others might take on some sort of temporary rental for a few days a week. Particularly adventurous Horses could suddenly crave their own camper van so they can take a home with them wherever they go!

Money follows these new opportunities in a very pleasing way, even if that Dragon wariness also extends to a few hold-ups in the cash actually reaching your bank account. Horses will also be successful in raising funds and taking on loans. Just don't exhaust Wood's generosity by demanding too much, too often. Also, take care with your spending, Horse. With all this Wood fuelling your flames, you're likely to burn through your fortune in record time.

The overseas travel theme carries on in your social life, Horse. As well as travel for business, many Horses will find themselves travelling for social occasions. Overseas weddings, family reunions, hen and stag parties, even family tree research could all demand you suddenly dust off your passport and join the fun.

Be prepared, too, for a surprise announcement from a friend. Looks like someone close could be planning something unexpected with you in mind, Horse. No, you'll never guess. You'll just have to wait and see.

All in all, your hooves will hardly touch the ground in 2024.

What it Means to Be a Horse

Sleek and graceful, as well as strong and swift, the Horse has always been an object of admiration and often longing. Young girls dream of having their own pony while many adults, on acquiring a pile of cash, often treat themselves to a racehorse or at least a share in one.

In China, the Horse is believed to be a symbol of freedom, and you've only got to see a picture of the famous white horses of the Camargue, exuberantly splashing through the marshes, to understand why.

People born in the year of the Horse exude a similar magnificence. They tend to be strong and athletic with broad shoulders and fine heads of thick hair. Where would the Horse be without its mane? Most Horses excel at sports, especially when young. They can run fast if they choose, but they will happily try any game until they find the one that suits them best.

Horses, being herd animals, are gregarious types and don't like to spend too long alone. They enjoying hanging out with a crowd, chatting and swapping gossip, and Horses of both sexes can lap up any amount of grooming. They love having their hair brushed and fussed over, their nails manicured; a facial or relaxing massage is usually welcome.

Yet, Horses are more complex than they first appear. The affable, easy-going charmer, delighting everyone at a party, can suddenly take offence at a casual remark or storm off in a huff over some tiny hitch almost unnoticeable to anyone else, leaving companions baffled. They tend to stay baffled too, because it's difficult to get a handle on what upsets the Horse since what annoys them one week may leave them completely unruffled the next.

The trouble is, although they look tough, Horses are, in fact, very sensitive. Inside, they're still half-wild. Their senses are incredibly sharp, and although they don't realise it, deep down they're constantly scanning the horizon and sniffing the air for the first signs of danger. As a result, Horses live on their nerves. They tend to over-react when things don't go completely to plan, and have to work hard to control a sense of panic. Ideally, Horses would like to bolt away when the going gets rough but as this is not usually possible, they get moody and difficult instead.

Provide calm, congenial conditions for a Horse, however, and you couldn't wish for a friendlier companion. The Horse is lively, enthusiastic, versatile, and fun.

At work, the Horse wants to do well but can't stand being fenced in or forced to perform repetitive, routine tasks. Also, although they're good in a team, Horses have a need for privacy and independence so they may change jobs frequently until they find the right role. Yet, when they're happy, Horses will shine.

At home, Horse is probably planning the next trip. Horses like to be comfortable but they're not the most domesticated of the signs. They love being in the open air and don't see the point of spending too much time wallowing on a sofa or polishing dusty ornaments. They may well spend more time in the garden than indoors. On holiday, Horse loves to head for wide-open spaces – a vast beach, a craggy hillside or a mountain meadow; Horse would be thrilled to explore them all.

Best Jobs for Horse

Riding Instructor

Runner

Dancer

Dog Trainer

PE Teacher

Sales Rep

Perfect Partners

Cupid's arrow can strike anywhere at any time, of course, but once the novelty of new romance wears off, some relationships are easier to maintain than others. Here's a guide to the Horse's compatibility with other signs.

Horse with Horse

No doubt about it, these two make a magnificent couple, and any foals in the family would be spectacular. They certainly understand each other, particularly their shared need for both company and alone time so, in general, they get on well. The only tricky part could come if they both grew anxious over the same issue at the same time. Neither would find it easy to calm the other.

Horse with Goat

Goat and Horse just click! These two love kicking up their heels and trotting off into the green. Goat doesn't need to go far or do anything strenuous but is always up for a break in routine, while Horse doesn't do routine at all so is constantly on the lookout for a partner ready to escape. This couple rarely considers the consequences but, mostly, they don't need to.

Horse with Monkey

Uh oh – best not attempted unless it's love at first sight. Monkey and Horse have wildly different outlooks and can't seem to see eye to eye on anything. They're both lively but in different ways that don't complement each other. Monkey will consider Horse's moods illogical and pointless while Horse is irritated that Monkey makes no attempt to understand how Horse feels. Very hard work.

Horse with Rooster

The eye-catching Rooster intrigues Horse while Rooster appreciates Horse's strength and agility. They can enjoy many stimulating dates together. Yet, in the long-run, this couple may not be able to provide the stability the other needs. They're both sensitive types but in different ways. After a while, the relationship could run out of steam.

Horse with Dog

Both good friends of man, these two can make a formidable team. Dog understands the occasional need for solitude while admiring Horse's strength and agility. Horse, meanwhile, senses Dog's loyalty and down to earth nature. Both lovers of the great outdoors and physical activity, they'll never be short of adventures to share. A promising long-term relationship.

Horse with Pig

Pig and Horse are good companions. Horse is soothed by easy-going Pig and Pig is proud to be seen with such an alluring creature as Horse. They don't have a lot of interests in common, but they don't antagonise each other either. They can jog along amicably for quite a while, but long-term they may find they each want more than the other can provide.

Horse with Rat

Rat and Horse both fizz with energy, and they love action and looking good, yet this is not seen as an ideal partnership. Nothing's impossible of course, but these two will have to work hard to find harmony. The Rat will admire Horse's enthusiasm and cheerful approach but become impatient to discover Horse can also be fiery and emotional. Horse, on the other hand, can find Rat's risk-taking behaviour extremely worrying.

Horse with Ox

Long ago on many Western farms, Ox was replaced by the Horse, and it may be that Ox has never forgotten and never forgiven. At any rate, these two, despite both being big, strong animals are not usually friends. Horse is too flighty and frivolous to interest Ox for long, while Ox's methodical, careful ways will irritate the Horse. Best not to go there.

Horse with Tiger

This athletic pair gets on pretty well. They both like physical pursuits, testing their strength out of doors or just enjoying the feel of the wind in their hair and the ground under their feet. True, Horse may not quite understand Tiger's plans for world domination, but it doesn't really matter. Horse is happy to be loyal to such a charismatic partner. As they're both moody, there could be rows but making up is exciting.

Horse with Rabbit

This could be tricky. It's fairly unlikely that Horse and Rabbit would ever end up on a date, but if they did and there was a strong attraction, it could lead to a love/hate relationship. Rabbit's neat and tidy ways would enrage Horse and Horse's unpredictable moods and over-the-top reactions would annoy Rabbit. Soon, Horse is likely to bolt for the hills or Rabbit retreat to its burrow.

Horse with Dragon

The athletic Horse is pretty good at keeping up with dashing Dragon. And Dragon appreciates a partner who enjoys getting out and about as much as Dragon does. Yet Horse might grow weary of Dragon's constant new projects and resent having to be involved. Horse likes to go off and do Horsey things at frequent intervals which Dragon tends to view as disloyal. This relationship could get fiery.

Horse with Snake

At some level, perhaps Horse remembers how Snake beat him in the calendar race, so despite an initial attraction, these two could be wary of each other. Snake is impressed by Horse's energy and athleticism, while Horse admires Snake's elegance and charm. Yet they don't really have much in common. Deep thinking Snake could find Horse rather shallow, and Horse may see Snake as frustratingly enigmatic.

Horse Love 2024 Style

Right now, you're more or less irresistible, Horse. Groomed and glossy for all those business meetings and job interviews, your classy appearance turns heads when the sun goes down, and you're off to play.

The truth is, though, you're so busy with travelling and career matters, you won't have a lot of time for romance. Single Horses are slightly hampered, too, by spending so much of their downtime in unfamiliar areas.

On the other hand, there will be no shortage of willing volunteers to show you around town. A mysterious stranger, particularly a stranger as alluring as you, Horse, is a very appealing prospect to bored locals. Chances are the single Horse will enjoy the variety.

Attached Horses have a different challenge. You'll need to take care your partner doesn't get jealous or resentful of those regular absences. It might be an idea to combine business with pleasure and take your love with you from time to time. Or maybe invest in that camper van and play gypsies on the open road.

Secrets of Success in 2024

Although the Dragon has a lot of time for you, Horse, a couple of your very minor tendencies are inclined to annoy the fire-breather. If you could dial these down in 2024, or even resist them entirely, your chances of success would skyrocket.

The main thing that irritates the Dragon is your occasional carelessness with work matters. Despite the Dragon always being up for fun, this is a creature that also takes business very seriously. Do it or don't do it, the Dragon believes, but if you take something on, you should give it your all. No wandering off in the middle because the task's become boring.

Fulfil your responsibilities properly, Horse, and the Dragon will reward you.

Then there's the other matter of your emotional nature, Horse. You must admit there are times, very few of course, when you could be accused of moodiness. Occasionally, your temper has a habit of flaring up quite unexpectedly, and this year, with all that Wood in the system, stoking your inner Fires into a furnace, you could be prone to reckless outbursts.

Play it cool in the face of whatever provocation comes your way, and you'll be a winner, Horse.

The Horse Year at a Glance

January – January blues could be getting you down, but cheer up; the Dragon will soon brighten your world and then some!

February – Things are hotting up. You can smell the change in the air. Exciting times are on the way.

March – An interesting career offer comes your way. Should you take it or wait for something better? Decision time.

April – Break out that suitcase. There's a trip this month most likely connected to work. You'll make a success of it.

May – A slight hitch to your plans slows you down. A misunderstanding, or is someone being deliberately obstructive? No matter, you'll trot past.

June – The boss is pleased with you. Looks like you're off again; keep on doing what you're doing.

July – Not much time for romance, but where there's a will, there's a way – and you find it!

August – A crazy friend tries to lure you into joining them on an adventure. It's certainly different, but why not?

September – A new boss or authority figure appears at work. Not a problem for you. You're flavour of the month.

October – An old friend reappears. The years roll away, and you pick up where you left off. Make time for repeat get-togethers.

November – the Horse coffers are swelling nicely, but so is your list of goodies to buy.

December – It can't be helped… you've made some money, so it's time to party. And your parties are legendary. Enjoy!

Lucky colours for 2024: Emerald Green, Orange, Gold

Lucky numbers for 2024: 7, 8, 2

Three Takeaways

Stay calm.

Try not to overreact.

Refuse to follow the crowd.

CHAPTER 5: THE GOAT

Goat Years

17 February 1931 – 5 February 1932

5 February 1943 – 24 January 1944

24 January 1955 – 11 February 1956

9 February 1967 – 29 January 1968

28 January 1979 – 15 February 1980

15 February 1991 – 3 February 1992

1 February 2003 – 21 January 2004

19 February 2015 – 7 February 2016

6 February 2027 – 25 January 2028

24 January 2039 – 11 February 2040

Natural Element: Fire

Will 2024 be a Golden Year for the Goat?

Are you ready, Goat? You may not suspect it yet, but you could be making your mark this year in a BIG way. It might be worth grabbing as much rest as you can in the next few weeks because life is about to get crazy.

If you're typical of your sign, Goat, you might greet this news with mixed feelings. You're a gentle type, very laid-back on the surface and very laid-back beneath the surface, too, as long as no one's rushing you. You're happy to go along with most things you're asked to do because you like to please, if possible, just so long as you can take your time. But if people try to hurry you, that's when stress sets in.

Despite being physically strong, the Goat's constitution is incredibly sensitive. Goats are the silent worriers of the zodiac, inwardly chewing over every tiny problem or unkind word. Upheavals, unpleasantness, or dramas – both good and bad – play havoc with the Goat's nerves.

Last year, under the soft-pawed rule of the Rabbit, most Goats tended to relax and unwind a little. They were able to start exploring new creative ideas, plant a few seeds and strike out in different, often unusual directions. Delightfully unexpected friendships began to take root. For the typical Goat, it was all coming together nicely at a calm, leisurely pace.

Well, stand by for a whirlwind now, Goat. Dragon doesn't really 'get' leisurely. Your prospects are excellent but not necessarily comfortable. The Dragon is there to help you right enough, but Dragon assistance can end up feeling overwhelming.

The trouble is the Dragon and the Goat are not natural buddies. It's not that they dislike each other, just that neither understands how the other operates. In fact, the Dragon in a hurry barely notices that Goat operates at all, so imperceptible is Goat's pace to Dragon's eyes.

Then there's the fact that this year is a Wood year and the Dragon is a Wood creature while the Goat is a Fire animal. Wood naturally feels a bit nervous around Fire since Fire is all-consuming as far as Wood is concerned. On the other hand, hungry Fire enjoys Wood and will gladly devour every last twig.

In day-to-day life, this see-saw quality could play out as a great many opportunities coming Goat's way, yet due to the Dragon's slight hesitancy, the opportunities dangle ever so slightly out of reach. Leap up and seize them, though, Goat – and Goats are expert leapers – and suddenly the opportunity opens up, expands and accelerates away like a forest fire after a six-month drought.

Employed Goats, business Goats, artist Goats, even student Goats will find themselves powering to success in 2024. Whether it's promotions, new clients, new orders or higher grades, typical Goats will find themselves showered with almost more than they can handle.

Artistic and horticultural Goats will fare best of all. Wood energy craves creation. Just make a start, Goat, and your project will take off like a rocket on New Year's Eve. Fame and fortune could well follow. Talents you hone in 2024 could lead to increased prosperity for years to come.

Talking of prosperity, cash will be flowing in this year, Goat, but it could flow out just as rapidly. Opportunities for spending will blossom all around. Many Goats will be inspired to remodel or extend their homes; Goat clans are likely to increase in all directions. From new kids to new partners with large clans of their own, the average Goat homestead will soon be bursting at the seams.

This is all delightful to the typical Goat. Goats are not overly motivated by money. While you don't like wasting cash, spending it on pretty things and your nearest and dearest seems like money well spent as far as the Goat is concerned.

Yet many Goats will be uneasy at all this mention of speed. Even in a good cause, the prospect of rushing might seem daunting. But there's good news here, too. With so much Wood energy flowing in the air, your Fiery constitution will get a boost every day. Suddenly, the typical Goat will be zinging with energy. You'll be amazed at the way you can burn through every task in record time. So, stop worrying! Whatever the Dragon throws your way, you can handle it.

What it Means to Be a Goat

If people born under the sign of the Goat tend to look a little puzzled, uncertain even, who could blame them? It's not even definite their sign is the Goat. Some authorities call their sign the Sheep. Others – the more macho types – have it down as the Ram.

The confusion seems to stem from different translations of the original Chinese word.

But what's in a name? Whatever you call it, the qualities ascribed to the Goat/Sheep/Ram are the same. In China, the sign is regarded as symbolising peace and harmony. What's more, it's the eighth sign of the zodiac and the number eight is believed to be a very lucky number, associated as it is with growth and prosperity.

So, all you confused Goats out there can relax in the knowledge you were born in a lucky year.

In truth, perhaps the gentle sheep – the living animal that is – does resemble the zodiac Goat more than the real-life goat. Flesh and blood goats tend to have a feisty, combative quality and a strongly stubborn streak. Those sharp, pointy horns and all that head-butting does tend to put people off.

Yet, people born in a Goat year are known as the sweetest and friendliest of all the signs. They possess no spikey quality at all. They are tolerant and kind, have no wish to be competitive, and want to see the best in everyone they meet. Though they may not realise it, this attitude often unconsciously brings out the best in others, so the Goat's expectations are usually fulfilled.

Goats seem to get on with almost everyone, even people that others can't abide.

What's more, Goats usually possess a wonderful artistic talent. Even those Goats who feel they can't paint, draw, or manage anything skilled, are nevertheless immensely creative with a fine eye for colour and design.

The Goat loves beautiful things and even sees beauty in objects and places that hold no appeal for others. They love to use their hands in their spare time, ideally making something practical yet decorative. Knitting, card-making, cake-decorating, gardening, or renovating old furniture, even DIY, will give them great pleasure.

Concepts such as time and also money, have little meaning for the Goat. When the Goat gets lost in inspiration, hours pass in seconds and Goat ends up late for anything else that might have been on the agenda.

Similarly, money is frustrating for the Goat. Goats are not materialistic; neither are they particularly ambitious in a worldly way. Objects other people regard as status symbols hold little Goat appeal so they can't see the point of putting in a lot of energy to acquire them. For this reason, Goats are not career-driven. All they really want to do is pursue their artistic project or latest interest. If this won't provide an income though, they'll do their best at whatever job turns up, in order to get back to their true vocation at weekends.

The perfect scenario for the Goat would be a big win on the lottery, so they never have to waste time on a conventional job again. Should this ever happen, they'd be advised to get someone else to look after the funds for them; Goats are not good at handling finances, and the windfall could slip through their fingers with distressing speed.

Goats are notoriously impractical with matters such as bills, household repairs, filling in forms, and meeting deadlines. They just can't seem to find the time to tackle such mundane items. Though they're intelligent people, they'll frequently claim not to understand such things. The truth is, of course, the ultra-creative Goat brain just can't be bothered.

One thing Goats do have in common with the flesh and blood animal is their stubborn streak. Despite that easy-going, sunny nature, zodiac Goats can astonish their friends by suddenly digging in their heels over what looks to others like a trivial matter of very little importance. Once Goat has adopted this position, it will not budge, no matter how unreasonable or how poor the outcome is likely to be.

The Goat home is an intriguing place. Striking and original, it's likely to be filled with mismatched treasures Goat has picked up along the way. Goats love car boot sales, junk shops, and galleries. They enjoy beach-combing and collecting branches and broken wood on country walks. They've even been known to 'rescue' items from rubbish skips. Somehow, Goat manages to weave together the most unpromising items to create a pleasing effect.

Best Jobs for Goat

Ceramicist

Jewellery Designer

Garden Designer

Early Years Teacher

Counsellor

Human Resources Manager

Perfect Partners

Cupid's arrow can strike anywhere at any time, of course, but once the novelty of new romance wears off, some relationships are easier to maintain than others. Here's a guide to the Goat's compatibility with other signs.

Goat with Goat

When things are going well, you won't find a happier couple than two Goats. They are perfectly in tune with each other's creative natures and understand when to do things together and when to step back and give the other space. And since they both share the same interests, their together times are always fun. Yet, when practical problems arise, neither can easily cope. With a helpful friend on speed-dial, this would work.

Goat with Monkey

Monkey and Goat are different but in a good way. Though they don't quite 'get' each other deep down, Goat admires Monkey's lively personality and magical ability to come up with solutions for everything, while curious Monkey enjoys Goat's knowledge of the arts and the unusual. Long-term, Goat might not present enough of a challenge for Monkey but, with effort, it's a promising match.

Goat with Rooster

Peaceful Goat is not one to make feathers fly, so these two are unlikely to fall out, but they're unlikely to find perfect compatibility either. Goat is unable to give Rooster the regular ego boosts that make Rooster thrive while Rooster is baffled by Goat's unpredictable devotion to impractical projects or people. Misunderstandings are likely.

Goat with Dog

This is another relationship that could be tricky. Loyal Dog would be quite willing to stand by Goat when practical problems loom but could end up irritated by Goat's inability to learn from previous mistakes and so keeps making them. Goat can't understand why Dog gets so bothered. With care, these two could learn to live together.

Goat with Pig

Happy-go-lucky Pig and laid-back Goat make a good pair. They hate to stir up trouble and always look for a peaceful solution to any challenge. Ideally, they'd avoid the challenge altogether. They could be very contented together as long as Pig's spending and Goat's inability to deal with finances doesn't get them into trouble.

Goat with Rat

The Rat is charmed by carefree Goat and fascinated by its artistic talent and happy knack of living in the present. Easy-going Goat tends to like everyone so is perfectly content to enjoy Rat's company. These two can get along fine, yet they don't really understand each other deep down. Long-term, the Rat may find Goat's lack of interest in the practical side of life irritating.

Goat with Ox

Though these two share artistic natures (even if in the case of the Ox, they're well hidden), deep down they don't 'get' one another. Ox may be beguiled at first by Goat's friendly, easy-going manner but then disappointed to discover Goat seems to find everyone equally delightful, even those who are plainly unworthy. Goat, on the other hand, can't understand why Ox won't lighten up more. This relationship would require a lot of effort and compromise.

Goat with Tiger

Tiger and Goat don't have a lot in common. While their aims and temperaments are quite different, they are both sociable creatures and Goat wouldn't mind Tiger attracting all the attention when they're out together. Tiger, in return, would appreciate Goat's lack of jealousy and generosity of spirit. Yet, long-term, they're likely to drift apart as they follow their different interests.

Goat with Rabbit

Wow! One glance across a crowded room and that's it for Goat and Rabbit. Rabbit instantly recognises and appreciates Goat's innate style and authenticity, while Goat admires Rabbit's restrained elegance and understated intellect. Both quiet, home-loving types, they also adore exploring and acquiring fine things. This couple will never be bored.

Goat with Dragon

Goat tends to baffle the busy Dragon. Dragon can see Goat is the creative type but can't understand why Goat doesn't appear to be working very hard when so much could be achieved. In fact, if they stayed together long enough, Dragon could help Goat make the most of many talents but it's unlikely either of them can sustain enough interest for this to happen.

Goat with Snake

Snake and Goat could enjoy many happy hours touring art galleries and exhibitions together. Neither of them craves excitement and harsh, adrenaline-boosting activities and both appreciate creative, artistic personalities. There's no pressure to compete with each other so these two would sail along quite contentedly. Not a passionate alliance but they could be happy.

Goat with Horse

Goat and Horse just click! These two love kicking up their heels and trotting off into the green. Goat doesn't need to go far or do anything strenuous but is always up for a break in routine, while Horse doesn't do routine at all so is constantly on the lookout for a partner ready to escape. This couple rarely considers the consequences, but mostly, they don't need to.

Goat Love 2024 Style

The amazing thing about you, Goat, is that since you get on with practically everyone, almost any available sign you encounter along the way is more than happy to give romance a whirl with you. Quite often, you weren't even thinking along those lines at all, but amiable as ever, you're not averse to hooking up to see how it goes.

Often, this approach works well, but sometimes you end up in tricky situations from which it's difficult to disentangle. Your new partner might not be as ready to move on as you are.

This year, you're hotter than ever, Goat. All that Wood energy is firing you up and single Goats are radiating sex appeal. You have a magnetic attraction that draws so many admirers from all directions you could get quite confused.

What's more, your social life gets a boost from that Wood energy, too, and for once, you're not too tired to take advantage of it! Stand by to be out almost every night, Goat, partying till dawn. You may not find your soulmate in 2024, but you'll certainly enjoy searching.

Attached Goats are not immune from the impulse to kick up their heels and party this year. This is fine as long as their partners feel the same way. If not, reasonable Goat sees no problem in taking off on their own while their beloved relaxes. Unfortunately, many a beloved sees differently. Jealousy and discord – most distressing to the Goat – could follow. Tread carefully.

Secrets of Success in 2024

There's no way round it, Goat, this year if you want the success you deserve, you've got to put in the effort. You always work hard, of course, you may protest, but the effort Dragon demands is consistent effort – with the emphasis on 'consistent'.

The typical Goat tends to drift between slaving intensely day and night, scarcely pausing even to eat, when inspired, and then lolling around for a week or two doing the barest minimum while they recover. This approach sometimes yields great results, but as far as the Dragon is concerned, there's a lot of wasted time that could be put to better use.

Organise your workload, Goat, think about restructuring your time in a more efficient way and you could be amazed at how much more you accomplish.

With the extra energy you've got on board in 2024, you're armed with all the tools you need to achieve more than you ever dreamed possible, Goat. So, get serious and get on!

The Goat Year at a Glance

January – It might be cold outside, but an unexpected gift will make you warm and happy.

February – Stand by for a reshuffle at work. A long-standing boss is on the way out. It could be good news.

March – Relief. The new boss thinks you're rather special. Just keep on doing what you're doing.

April – Spring flowers are appearing, and your creative juices are flowing. Something splendid could evolve.

May – An intriguing offer comes your way – maybe connected to an artistic venture. Consider it carefully.

June – An early break is in the wind, yet you're not sure whether to accept. A friend will be disappointed if you back out.

July – Look out for a whirlwind romance. Loving eyes have noticed you. Have you noticed them?

August – A complicated person is trying to blind you with science. Don't get stressed. Keep calm and trust your common sense.

September – Good news, Goat, a financial boost is on the way. Pay rise or winnings or maybe a gift? Enjoy.

October – Another new face at work could ruffle feathers. New rules and regulations cause friction. Keep out of it, Goat.

November – Time to lighten up. An old friend wants to go shopping, and you know how to shop! Try not to max out those cards, Goat.

December – Party time is back again, and you've gone a bit crazy with the gifts. You'll have a ball.

Lucky colours for 2024: Green, Purple, Silver.

Lucky numbers for 2024: 7, 5, 1

Three Takeaways

Go a little crazy – experiment.

Create a private sanctuary.

Have confidence. Your gifts are unique.

CHAPTER 6: THE MONKEY

Monkey Years

6 February 1932 – 25 January 1933

25 January 1944 – 12 February 1945

12 February 1956 – 30 January 1957

30 January 1968 – 16 February 1969

16 February 1980 – 4 February 1981

4 February 1992 – 22 January 1993

22 January 2004 – 8 February 2005

8 February 2016 – 27 January 2017

26 January 2028 – 12 February 2029

12 February 2040 – 31 January 2041

Natural Element: Metal

Will 2024 be a Golden Year for the Monkey?

Congratulations, Monkey! You, along with your fellow sign the Rat, are joint winners of the most favoured creature of 2024 competition. Okay, so maybe it wasn't actually a competition, but it might as well have been. The other members of the celestial zodiac would gladly have challenged you for the privilege if they could.

So, what did you do to achieve such good fortune, you might be wondering? To be honest, Monkey, nothing much other than just being your intriguing, entertaining self.

The Dragon adores the Monkey. Can't help it. The two of you get on wonderfully well. You're the very best of friends. So, when the Dragon's running things, everyone born under the sign of the Monkey gets preferential treatment.

Last year might have been slow-going for you, Monkey, because the Rabbit in charge of 2023 was a bit fussy and picky for your taste. Many a Monkey found they couldn't get on with things the way they hoped. They had to keep going back to sort out silly details, or take the official, long way around instead of finding a short cut.

Hold-ups and minor obstacles were simply the result of you and the Rabbit not being naturally compatible. You're not hostile to each other, but you're not totally approving either, which causes a certain amount of friction.

Well, say goodbye to irritations and pointless (in Monkey eyes) rules and regulations, Monkey. This year, you'll sail through. If you ever fancied starting a business, going self-employed, or maybe retraining for a completely different career altogether, 2024 is the year to give it a go.

Your brilliant brain has probably got a million original and ingenious ideas just clamouring to be put into practice. Get them started, and the Dragon will breathe them into vibrant life. The more innovative, the better. The Dragon enjoys wild and whacky, so don't hold back; you may never get a chance this good again.

Employed Monkeys are likely to become the boss's pet – much to the envy of the rest of the staff. Monkey opinions are sought after and taken seriously. Monkey suggestions once regarded as eccentric or impractical are suddenly hailed as sheer brilliance. Many a Monkey will even find themselves invited to socialise with the boss and impress authority figures with their charm.

The Monkey bank account is likely to benefit from the same good fortune and expansion, and if you're a typical Monkey, you're likely to end up making some unusual purchases this year.

Some sort of futuristic car or quirky classic version could suddenly leap to the top of the primate shopping list. If coffers permit, many a Monkey could be tempted by a novel holiday home – lighthouse, anyone? Gypsy caravan complete with pony?

But Monkeys with less cash to spare will make do with a radical new look, or maybe several.

The only slight awkwardness that could arise can be attributed to the fact that 2024 is a Wood year, and the Dragon being a Wood creature only magnifies the prevailing woodiness. The trouble is, the Monkey is a Metal animal, and this is a difficult combination since Metal is associated with sharp, cutting objects such as axes, which can do Wood a great deal of harm. Not surprisingly, Wood creatures usually prefer to keep out of Metal's way.

The Dragon makes an exception for the Monkey, of course, but with so much wood energy in the air, nevertheless, Monkey plans could be affected by certain baffling hesitancy now and then. This could materialise in day-to-day life as a tendency for new friends and business associates to 'blow hot and cold' for no reason. Full of enthusiasm one minute, then suddenly changing their minds. Fortunately, they're just as likely to change them back again under the influence of the Dragon, so it shouldn't be too much of a problem.

It looks like you're going to enjoy 2024!

What it Means to be a Monkey

There was a time when we tended to regard the Monkey as a figure of fun. The creature's awesome agility, effortless acrobatics, and natural clowning made us laugh, and if they sensed an audience, the animals would show off shamelessly. Which, of course, only made us enjoy them more.

Yet, in China, the Monkey was credited with far more qualities than merely those of a born entertainer. The sign of the Monkey is associated with intelligence, justice, and wisdom. Behind those mischievous eyes, the Chinese detected a shrewd brain and ability to plan the best course of action.

Like their namesakes, people born under the sign of Monkey tend to be physically agile. They're quick-moving, quick-thinking types with glittering wit and charismatic personalities. At a party, the Monkey will be in the centre of the group that's convulsed with laughter. Monkeys love jokes and humour of all kinds, and if anyone's going to start entertaining the crowd with a few magic tricks, it's likely to be a Monkey.

While not necessarily conventionally good-looking, the Monkey's lively face and sparkling eyes are always attractive, and Monkeys have no difficulty in acquiring partners. The tricky bit for a Monkey is staying around long enough to build a relationship.

People born under this sign need constant mental stimulation. They don't necessarily expect others to provide it. They are quite happy to amuse themselves with puzzles, conundrums, the mending of broken objects, and inventing things, but they also need new places and new faces. Few signs can keep up with Monkey's constant motion.

What's more, Monkeys are not good with rules or authority. They've seldom seen a rule they don't want to break or avoid. In fact, it sometimes seems as if Monkey deliberately seeks out annoying regulations just for the fun of finding a way around them.

Yet, beneath the humour and games, the Monkey is ambitious with an astute brain. Monkeys can turn their hand to almost anything and make a success of it, but they're probably best-suited to working for themselves. If anyone is going to benefit from their efforts they believe it should be, chiefly, themselves. Also, they're not good at taking orders and, to be fair, they're so clever they don't need to. They can usually see the best way to carry out a task better than anyone else.

The Monkey home is often a work in progress. Monkey is always looking for a quicker, easier, cheaper, or more efficient way of doing everything and new ideas could encompass the entire building from the plumbing to the lighting and novel security systems. The first home in the street to be operated by remote control is likely to be the Monkey's. Yet, chances are, Monkey would prefer to meet friends in a nearby restaurant.

When it comes to holidays, Monkeys can have a bag packed seemingly in seconds, and are ready to be off anywhere, anytime. They don't much mind where they go as long as it's interesting, unusual, and offers plenty to be discovered. Lying on a sun-lounger for extended periods does not appeal.

Best Jobs for Monkey 2024

Athlete

Diplomat

Magician

Inventor

Public Relations

Actor

Sports Promoter

Perfect Partners

Cupid's arrow can strike anywhere at any time, of course, but once the novelty of new romance wears off, some relationships are easier to maintain than others. Here's a guide to the Monkey compatibility with other signs.

Monkey with Monkey

It's not always the case that opposites attract. More often, like attracts like and when two Monkeys get together, they find each other delightful. At last, they've met another brain as quick and agile as their own and a person who relishes practical jokes as much as they do. What's more, this is a partner that shares a constant need for change and novelty. Yet, despite this, two Monkeys can often end up competing with each other. As long as they can recognise this, and laugh about it, they'll be fine.

Monkey with Rooster

While not a perfect match, these two have got a lot of time for each other. Monkey recognises the intelligent brain beneath Rooster's plumage while Rooster admires Monkey's ability to entertain a crowd and they both adore socialising. They could enjoy many fun dates together. Long-term, though, Rooster may tire of Monkey's jokes.

Monkey with Dog

Monkey finds Dog intriguing. Monkey senses Dog's strength of character coupled with its playful streak, which fits well with Monkey's love of games. Dog, meanwhile, appreciates Monkey's energy and light-hearted approach. Yet, before long, Monkey's disdain for rules will grate on Dog's instinctive love of them. They cannot agree in this area, and it could lead to arguments.

Monkey with Pig

On the surface, these two might seem an unlikely couple. Yet Pig enjoys Monkey's fun and humour while Monkey is happy to be admired uncritically. What's more, Monkey's inventive mind can solve any difficulties caused by Pig's spending and since Monkey can't resist a challenge, the opportunity to retrain Pig, or at least find a way to obtain purchases cheaper, could help the relationship last.

Monkey with Rat

Unlikely as it might appear, mischievous Monkey and the clever Rat make a good partnership. Their quick minds, sociable natures, and love of novelty ensure that they're never bored together. True, Rat might sometimes feel that Monkey is too inclined to skim over the surface of things and could do with being more serious at times, but Monkey's ingenuity and audaciousness always saves the day. Both can have a weakness for gambling though, so need to take care.

Monkey with Ox

The naughty Monkey scandalises Ox but in such an amusing way that Ox can't help laughing. Monkey, on the other hand, is equally amused to find an audience so easy to shock. This unlikely pair enjoy each other's company and get on surprisingly well. Yet, right from the start, it's probably obvious to both that a long-term relationship couldn't last. A fun flirtation, though, could be a terrific tonic for them both.

Monkey with Tiger

Tiger can't help being intrigued by sparkling Monkey and Monkey is flattered by such interest. Who wouldn't enjoy being admired by such a fabulous creature? But irrepressible Monkey just can't help teasing, and being teased is not a sensation Tiger is familiar with (or appreciates). Unless the attraction is very strong, these two will wind each other up until they can bear it no longer and part.

Monkey with Rabbit

Mercurial Monkey doesn't really 'get' Rabbit. The Monkey can appreciate how well Rabbit operates and sees this approach gets good results, but it's all too picky and slow for Monkey. Rabbit, on the other hand, is amused by Monkey's quick wit and clever ways but deplores Monkey's slapdash, sometimes devious tactics. Very unlikely to work out.

Monkey with Dragon

These two are likely to hit it off immediately. Each is attracted to the other's intelligence and lively presence, and Dragon's exuberance doesn't overwhelm hyperactive Monkey. What's more, although they both enjoy being surrounded by a crowd, Monkey only wants to make people laugh while Dragon hopes to inspire them to a cause. There is no conflict, so this couple can help each other to go far.

Monkey with Snake

These two clever creatures ought to admire each other, if only for their fine minds and, at first, it's possible they might. But unless they're really determined to make it work, it won't be long before active Monkey finds Snake's energy-saving ways irritating, while Snake loses patience with Monkey's endless jokes.

Monkey with Horse

Uh oh – best not attempted unless it's love at first sight. Monkey and Horse have wildly different outlooks and can't seem to see eye to eye on anything. They're both lively but in different ways that don't complement each other. Monkey will consider Horse's moods illogical and pointless while Horse is irritated that Monkey makes no attempt to understand how Horse feels. Very hard work.

Monkey with Goat

Monkey and Goat are different but in a good way. Though they don't quite 'get' each other deep down, Goat admires Monkey's lively personality and magical ability to come up with solutions for everything, while curious Monkey enjoys Goat's knowledge of the arts and the unusual. Long-term, Goat might not present enough of a challenge for Monkey but, with effort, it's a promising match.

Monkey Love 2024 Style

Naughty Monkey. After an exciting love life last year, if you're typical of your sign, you'll be pleased to hear romance is looking for you once again.

Dragon power is shimmering around the Monkey, bathing all primates in a spectacular glow. Single Monkeys only have to step into a room to attract every eye with their sparkling allure. Of course, once you're the centre of attention, Monkey, you just can't help performing. And as you well know, when you're on top form, no one can resist your witty charm. Admirers fall at your feet, and you simply have to take your pick.

Attached Monkeys could enjoy a fabulous 2024 with their partner. Just direct the full force of that charm on your beloved for a change, and you'll enjoy the honeymoon effect all year.

Secrets of Success in 2024

Well, basically, Monkey, more or less all you have to do to succeed in 2024 is show up. The Dragon is waiting in the wings, just itching to propel your plans rapidly to wherever you'd like them to go, while the Wood energy of the year is poised to help them flourish when they get there.

Yet perversely – and you do have a slight perverse streak, Monkey – you could still snatch failure from the jaws of success if you begin to take your good fortune for granted.

Much as the Dragon loves you, Dragons do tend to be serious about work. Having a laugh while you go about your business is fine with Dragon. It is encouraged even. But get a little arrogant, begin to assume you don't really need to bother, and the indulgent Dragon can suddenly turn a little fiery.

This could play out in day-to-day life as tempting offers suddenly being withdrawn, well-laid plans turning to ashes, or previously enthusiastic colleagues and associates going cold on you.

Try to show a little humility, Monkey. Adopt a grateful attitude, and a brilliant year is assured.

The Monkey Year at a Glance

January – Here comes the Dragon! You can sense the impending change. A big shot of energy obliterates the January blues.

February – You're in the mood for dancing. Dragon celebrations Chez Monkey seem like a wonderful idea.

March – Changes at work look intriguing. Secrets are revealed, and there are consequences. But not for you.

April – Monkeys are flavour of the month everywhere. Time to start something new.

May – A devious person in your circle shows their true colours. You outsmart them with ease.

June – Romance is simmering. Juggling a jealous love with a new face could prove challenging – but then you love a challenge.

July – Old friends descend. It's time to get out and about and enjoy a reunion.

August – Cash is pouring into the Monkey bank, and you have a hundred ways to spend it.

September – Someone in your circle is arranging a surprise party. Could it be for you? If not, make sure your lips stay sealed.

October – Business projects are doing well, but resist the temptation for jokes and pranks. Certain elements around you now lack a sense of humour.

November – Authority figures turn very fond of you this month. An unusual invitation arrives.

December – Stand by for stellar festivities. Good news in the family circle delights everyone.

Lucky colours for 2024: Silver, Emerald Green, Yellow

Lucky numbers for 2024: 8, 2

Three Takeaways

Enjoy yourself but don't overdo it.

Make allowances for slower minds.

Test the branch before you leap.

CHAPTER 7: THE ROOSTER

Rooster Years

26 January 1933 – 13 February 1934

13 February 1945 – 1 February 1946

31 January 1957 – 17 February 1958

17 February 1969 – 5 February 1970

5 February 1981 – 24 January 1982

23 January 1993 – 9 February 1994

9 February 2005 – 28 January 2006

28 January 2017 – 15 February 2018

13 February 2029 – 2 February 2030

1 February 2041 – 21 January 2042

Natural Element: Metal

Will 2024 be a Golden Year for the Rooster?

Wow, Rooster! The time has come to drag out your showiest outfit, do something spectacular with your hair, and get yourself out there where you can be seen.

In 2024, you're set to make an impression. And then some.

While 2023's cuddly Rabbit was settling your nerves after the bashing they've probably received over the last few years, most Roosters were happy to sit back, keep a low profile, and quietly rebuild their lives.

But now, if you're typical of your sign, the pieces are more or less back in place, if not exactly the same place they were before the various upheavals began.

There's no longer any excuse to hide away. The Dragon doesn't do shy and retiring, and in a Dragon year neither should you!

Things are definitely looking up for the Rooster prospects. For a start, the Dragon rather likes Roosters. The two of you, while not quite total besties, get along pretty well. When you're at your boldest best, the Dragon admires your vibrant style.

The point is, the Dragon would now like to see a whole lot more of it. 2024 is not the year to be a faint-hearted, Rooster. Strike out fearlessly in adventurous new directions, and the results will be phenomenal.

This year, you're being encouraged to focus on your career, on business opportunities, and on generally enlarging your current circle. If there's an interest or hobby you've always fancied pursuing, add that to the list as well.

You don't need to worry about your stamina. There's more energy on offer for you in 2024, too. The last couple of years have been awash with the Water element, which can be very tiring for Metal creatures such as yourself, Rooster. This is because Metal is believed to nurture Water, which is lovely for Water but can get pretty exhausting for Metal after a while. So, you may have become used to feeling inexplicably fatigued and reckon it's your normal state of affairs these days.

Not so. This year, the water has finally drained away, releasing you from many vitality-sapping obligations, and leaving you free to rediscover your old vigour.

The new Wood element of 2024 is not quite without its own challenges, of course. This is because Wood is not entirely relaxed around Metal, with its unfortunate associations with sharp, cutting implements such as axes.

In everyday life, this slight unease could manifest as a certain hesitancy on the part of new friends and colleagues to commit themselves to Rooster projects, and promised finance could be slow to arrive.

Nevertheless, don't give up, Rooster. All will come right in the end. In fact, many Roosters will end up being the boss before 2025 comes around.

2024 sees the completion of various issues begun in previous years and the start of exciting new ventures. Many Roosters will find themselves inspired to dust off an idea from the past, reimagine it from a fresh angle, and actually launch it properly this time. Do this, Rooster, and Dragon energy will lend your brainwave wings. Fame and fortune could swiftly follow.

Cash may not be flowing in and out quite as quickly as it did in the previous Water years, but under the Wood influence, you'll see what you have, then grow and expand in a very pleasing way.

All in all, the typical Rooster will enjoy a very busy year. You seem to be in demand from every side – at work, socially and in the family circle. Everyone wants a Rooster to liven things up. Expect a great many parties and festive gatherings in 2024, Rooster, as well as a particular cause for celebration. And stand by to visit an exciting place you've never been before. Once you've checked this place out, you'll return many times. Enjoy.

What it Means to be a Rooster

Colourful, bold, and distinctly noisy, the Rooster rules the farmyard. Seemingly fearless and relishing the limelight, this bird may be small, but he doesn't appear to know it. We're looking at a giant personality here. This creature may be the bane of late sleepers, and only a fraction of the size of other animals on the farm, but the Rooster doesn't care. Rooster struts around, puffing out his tiny chest as if he owns the place.

The Chinese associate the Rooster with courage, and it's easy to see why. You'd have to be brave to square up to all-comers armed only with a modest beak, a couple of sharp claws, and a piercing shriek. Yet, Rooster is quite prepared to take on the challenge.

People born in the year of the Rooster tend to be gorgeous to look at, and like to dress flamboyantly. Even if their physique is not as slender as it could be, the Rooster is not going to hide it away in drab, black outfits. Roosters enjoy colour and style, and they dress to be noticed. These are not shy retiring types. They like attention, and they do whatever they can to get it.

Roosters are charming and popular with quick minds and engaging repartee. They have to guard against a tendency to boast, but this happens mainly when they sense a companion's interest is wandering. And since they're natural raconteurs, they can usually recapture attention and pass their stories off as good entertainment.

Like the feathered variety, Roosters can be impetuous and impulsive. They tend to rush into situations and commitments that are far too demanding, without a second thought and then, later on, wonder frantically how they're going to manage. Oddly enough, they usually make things work but only after ferocious effort. Roosters just can't help taking a risk.

Although they're gregarious and often surrounded by friends, there's a sense that – deep down – few people know the real Rooster. Underneath the bright plumage and cheerful banter, Rooster is quite private and a little vulnerable. Perhaps Roosters fear they'll disappear or get trampled on if they don't make enough noise. So, they need frequent reassurance that they're liked and appreciated.

With all the emphasis Rooster puts on the splendid Rooster appearance, it's often overlooked that, in fact, the Rooster has a good brain and is quite a thinker. Roosters keep up with current affairs, they're shrewd with money and business matters, and though you never see them doing it, in private they're busily reading up on all the latest information on their particular field.

At work, Rooster wants to be the boss and often ends up that way. Failing that, Roosters will go it alone and start their own business. They're usually successful due to the Rooster's phenomenal hard work, but when things do go wrong, it's likely to be down to the Rooster's compulsion to take a risk or promise more than it's possible to deliver. Also, while being sensitive to criticism, themselves, Roosters can be extremely frank in putting across their views to others. They may pride themselves on their plain-speaking, but it may not do them any favours with customers and employees.

Rooster thinks the home should be a reflection of its owner's splendid image so, if at all possible, it will be lavish, smart, and full of enviable items. They have good taste, in a colourful way, and don't mind spending money on impressive pieces. If the Rooster can be persuaded to take a holiday, a five-star hotel in a prestigious location with plenty of socialising would be ideal, or a luxury cruise with a place at the Captain's Table.

Best Jobs for Rooster 2024

Lecturer

TV Presenter

Politician

Charity Boss

Vintage Clothes Business

Classic Car Dealer

Perfect Partners

Cupid's arrow can strike anywhere at any time, of course, but once the novelty of new romance wears off, some relationships are easier to maintain than others. Here's a guide to the Rooster's compatibility with other signs.

Rooster with Rooster

Fabulous to look at though they would be, these two alpha creatures would find it difficult to share the limelight. They can't help admiring each other at first sight, but since both needs to be the boss, there could be endless squabbles for dominance. What's more, neither would be able to give the other the regular reassurance they need. Probably not worth attempting.

Rooster with Dog

Rooster and Dog are not the best of partners. Dog can be as plain-spoken as Rooster and is not likely to be impressed by overt show. What's more, Dog is often critical, and Rooster can't stand criticism. Rooster, on the other hand, is likely to sense and resent Dog's attitude. Frustration abounds for both in this relationship. Only for the hopelessly love-struck.

Rooster with Pig

These two might seem an unlikely couple – modest Pig with extrovert Rooster. Yet Pig has no need or wish to crow and can see the vulnerable character that lurks beneath Rooster's fine feathers; Rooster, meanwhile, responds to Pig's kindness and undemanding nature. As long as Rooster doesn't get bored, this can be a contented relationship.

Rooster with Rat

The first thing Rat notices about the Rooster is its beautiful plumage, but this is a relationship which is unlikely to get much further than initial admiration. Rooster's direct and frank approach can strike the Rat as tactless, while the Rooster can't understand why Rat has to make life so convoluted and complicated. Then again, Rooster's natural confidence and aplomb can come across as bragging to the Rat. These two have to be very determined to make a partnership work.

Rooster with Ox

For all its bravado and showing off, the Rooster is a down-to-earth type, drawn to security and accumulating the good things in life – requirements that Ox understands very well and can supply effortlessly. What's more, Ox can't help but admire Rooster's fine feathers and skill at communicating in a crowd – attributes Ox doesn't have and is unlikely to acquire. These two could enjoy a very good partnership.

Rooster with Tiger

The only feathered creature in the zodiac, the opulence and novelty of Rooster's appearance will draw Tiger like a magnet. What's more, deep down they are both quite serious-minded types so on one level they'll have much to share. Yet, despite this, they're not really on the same wavelength and misunderstandings will keep recurring. Could be hard work.

Rooster with Rabbit

A difficult match. However unfair it seems, Rooster comes over as loud, boastful, and uncouth to Rabbit while Rabbit appears dull, staid, and insufficiently admiring of Rooster's fine feathers to appeal to Rooster. These two just can't see below the surface of the other and it would be surprising if they ended up together. Only to be considered by the very determined.

Rooster with Dragon

A Dragon and Rooster pairing will always attract attention. These two are both gorgeous beings and love to be surrounded by admirers. They will probably enjoy going out together and being seen as a couple, but in the long-term they may not be able to provide the kind of support each secretly needs. Entertaining for a while but probably not a lasting relationship.

Rooster with Snake

Surprisingly, Snake and Rooster work well together. Both gorgeous in different ways, they complement each other without competing. Snake's keen eyes can see beneath Rooster's proud facade to the sensitive, unsure person inside, while Rooster appreciates Snake's unobtrusive strength and wise words of encouragement at just the right moment. These two could be inseparable.

Rooster with Horse

The eye-catching Rooster intrigues Horse while Rooster appreciates Horse's strength and agility. They can enjoy many stimulating dates together. Yet, in the long-run, this couple may not be able to provide the stability the other needs. They're both sensitive types but in different ways. After a while, the relationship could run out of steam.

Rooster with Goat

Peaceful Goat is not one to make feathers fly, so these two are unlikely to fall out, but they're unlikely to find perfect compatibility either. Goat is unable to give Rooster the regular ego boosts that make Rooster thrive while Rooster is baffled by Goat's unpredictable devotion to impractical projects or people. Misunderstandings are likely.

Rooster with Monkey

While not a perfect match, these two have got a lot of time for each other. Monkey recognises the intelligent brain beneath Rooster's plumage while Rooster admires Monkey's ability to entertain a crowd and they both adore socialising. They could enjoy many fun dates together. Long-term, though, Rooster may tire of Monkey's jokes.

Rooster Love 2024 Style

The only thing that could be slightly lacking in this splendid year is your love life, Rooster. Not that there's anything wrong with your romantic prospects. Romance is all around you. It's just that many a single Rooster could end up looking back over 2024 and say, 'What Romance?'

You're looking dazzling, Rooster, and you'll certainly get yourself noticed. You will also be radiating a highly attractive air of optimism and confidence. Partners will be there for the picking. It's just that you're so busy and excited by everything else going on in your life, you'll scarcely notice them.

Single Roosters interested in hooking up with someone special this year would do well to keep some slots in the diary. And if someone intriguing gives you their number, make sure you call them. Don't lose it or tell yourself you can't find the time.

Attached Roosters are likely to enjoy fine weekends with their partners, though not necessarily in a fairy-tale romance kind of way. The two of you could find yourselves working or planning something exciting together: a house move, unusual holiday, joint business venture or maybe an exploration of some kind. Whatever it is, the two of you will adore dreaming the details, and getting closer and closer as you dream.

Secrets of Success in 2024

There's no doubt you've got everything going for you this year, Rooster. In 2024, you really could cruise your way to success faster than at any time in ages. In fact, you probably can't even remember a year when your prospects were better.

Yet it's still possible to fail to make the most of the opportunities the Dragon will present. Mainly due to one small, annoying characteristic of yours. Confidence. Or rather, a lack of it.

Roosters are rightly famed for their courage, but courage is not the same as confidence. Few people realise that beneath those jaunty feathers and bold words, the typical Rooster sometimes struggles with a sense of not being good enough.

So, this year, should colleagues be slow to show enthusiasm for a Rooster plan, should necessary permissions hang too long in the balance, or should a new venture plod rather than race from the starting line, it's all too easy for the Rooster to give up the whole silly idea and walk away.

You've been here before, Rooster – giving up too soon when you could have accomplished much. So, make 2024 the year you hold your head up high when the going gets tough, when you refuse to deviate from your path for any obstacle, when you just keep on going, one foot in front of the other until you reach your goal.

You can do it, Rooster. And you'll find success.

The Rooster Year at a Glance

January – The Year of the Rabbit is easing away, and you toast its passing with good friends.

February – Someone picky at work fails to get into the new Dragon spirit. Everyone's tiptoeing around. You don't have to join them.

March – Things are lightening up. You treat yourself to a new look. Maybe the Rooster homestead wants sprucing, too.

April – The year's getting better and better. A new project at work has your name on it. You can make things happen.

May – Just when you wondered if you'd taken on too much, a wise person steps in with encouragement.

June – A leaving do or farewell party in the Rooster street turns out to be surprisingly enjoyable. A secret could be revealed.

July – Someone is not pulling their weight. You don't like confrontations, but they need to be told. If you can't delegate, be brave.

August – A bestie or cherished partner suggests a fun time. You're probably having fun already, but go with the flow.

September – A cash windfall makes your month. They could be winnings of some sort. Make the most.

October – You're in the mood to party, but there's a misery in your circle. Don't let them spoil the moment. Sidestep diplomatically.

November – Work is super busy, but you find a way to zoom through in record time. Much praise from on high.

December – Things are going so well you're almost sorry it's the hols. Almost, but not quite! Extra sparkling festivities Chez Rooster this year.

Lucky colours for 2024: Silver, Peach, White

Lucky numbers for 2024: 9, 1, 3

Three Takeaways

Avoid negative people.

Ignore criticism.

Trust your instincts.

CHAPTER 8: THE DOG

Dog Years

14 February 1934 – 3 February 1935

2 February 1946 – 21 January 1947

18 February 1958 – 7 February 1959

6 February 1970 – 26 January 1971

25 January 1982 – 12 February 1983

10 February 1994 – 30 January 1995

29 January 2006 – 17 February 2007

16 February 2018 – 4 February 2019

13 February 2029 – 2 February 2030

22 January 2042 – 9 February 2043

Natural Element: Metal

Will 2024 be a Golden Year for the Dog?

The great thing about you, Dog, if you're typical of your sign, is that you love a challenge. In fact, without a challenge, it's sometimes difficult to rouse yourself to achieve the excellent things of which you're more than capable. Some of your greatest successes have occurred when you've risen so far above an awkward challenge that you've practically soared into the stratosphere.

So, the good news is that 2024 is set to bring you more challenges than the last two years, along with more opportunities to improve your life in a big way.

The change in outlook for the typical Dog has come about because for – the past two years – the zodiac animals running events, the Tiger of 2022 and the Rabbit of 2023, are both pretty good friends of the Dog. This meant that most Dogs had a reasonably smooth run back then. Of course, there were challenges and the odd disappointment (no year is without them), but if you were typical of your sign, you should have fared better than quite a few of your cosmic cousins.

What happens in the reign of the Dragon of 2024 is an abrupt change of atmosphere. The Dragon and the Dog just don't care for each other. It's not so much that their personalities clash, more that they don't get close enough even to squabble. Neither understands the other.

On top of that, this is a Wood year, and the Dragon is a Wood creature, while the Dog belongs to the Metal family. True, Metal is unfazed by harmless Wood, but Wood is distinctly uneasy around Metal with its connection to any number of sharp objects that could cause serious harm to Wood.

So, the ruler of the year is not naturally in sympathy with the Dog, and neither is the element. Not exactly a promising start, you might think. But there's no need to despair, Dog. This bracing atmosphere is just the impetus you need to shake yourself out of that comfortable inertia and make things happen. You possess all the qualities you need to overcome any disadvantage. In fact, if you're smart, you can make 2024 one of your best years ever.

You have several important factors going for you. For a start, the Dragon brings fair and generous energy. So, while you won't be singled out for preferential treatment, if you earn rewards, the Dragon will make sure you receive them.

The Dragon also approves of hard work and a bold, courageous approach. And while you love to snooze in front of a warm fire or bask in the sun as much as anyone when you get the chance, Dog, when you've made up your mind to start work, few labour as long and hard as you do. As for courage, there's no one braver, particularly if home and family are at risk.

So, there's no need to fear the Dragon. As for the Wood element – while it might not be comfortable around you, you will benefit like everyone else from the growth and expansion on offer.

For employed Dogs, this plays out in everyday life as the need to put in extra effort to impress the boss. Business Dogs and self-employed Dogs will have to dream up more creative and audacious ways to attract clients. But get the new approach right, and you will prosper as never before.

Some Dogs could throw a tantrum under the pressure, of course, and stomp off to try a whole new career. Yet, once again, this is actually for the best. It's only what they should have done years ago. All these moves are ultimately beneficial to Dog interests.

At home, too, many Dogs could find themselves dissatisfied in some way with their accommodation. Perhaps this has not been ideal for quite a while, but suddenly – in 2024 – the typical Dog will either decide enough's enough and start looking for alternatives, or a move could be forced on them.

Either way, though uncomfortable for a while, if you're typical of your sign, Dog, you'll end up very glad you roused yourself to make the change. The new Dog abode will work far better for you, and unexpected benefits will unfold as the months wear on.

Then there's that family of yours and your friends. Friction is likely to arise in many a Dog circle. Once again, no one likes friction, but it seems that many Dogs have been putting up with behaviour that's unacceptable, or they've allowed people to take advantage of their good nature. The tension opens your eyes, Dog, and you finally decide to put your foot down.

This is likely to cause tempers to fray. Huffs could develop with certain family members, and some friends may disappear, but again, when the dust settles, the typical Dog will enjoy happier, healthier relationships all around.

And the good news is the Dog extended family is likely to expand and expand this year. New puppies, new partners, even new pets are set to join the canine household in the coming months, bringing great joy to you all.

What it Means to be a Dog

Though some cultures are quite rude about the dog, and regard the very name as a disparaging term, in the West, we tend to be rather sentimental about our canine friends.

The Chinese, on the other hand, while regarding the zodiac Dog with respect, discern more weighty qualities in the faithful hound. They regard the sign of the Dog as representing justice and compassion. People born under the sign of the Dog, therefore, are admired for their noble natures and fair-minded attitudes.

Typical Dogs will do the right thing, even if it means they'll lose out personally. They have an inbuilt code of honour that they hate to break.

The Dog is probably the most honest sign of the zodiac. People instinctively trust the Dog even if they don't always agree with Dog's opinions. Yet Dogs are usually completely unaware of the high esteem in which they're held, because they believe they're only acting naturally; doing what anyone else would do in the circumstances.

Since they have such a highly-developed sense of right and wrong, Dogs understand the importance of rules. Also, since deep down they're always part of a pack – even if it's invisible – Dogs know that fairness is vital. If there aren't fair shares all round, there's likely to be trouble they believe. So, to keep the peace, Dog knows that a stout framework of rules is required and once set up, everyone should stick to them. Dogs are genuinely puzzled that other signs can't seem to grasp this simple truth!

People born under this sign tend to be physically strong with thick, glossy hair, and open, friendly faces. Their warm manner attracts new acquaintances, but they tend to stay acquaintances for quite a while. It takes a long time for Dog to promote a person from acquaintance to real friend. This is because Dogs are one hundred percent loyal and will never let a friend down, so they don't give their trust lightly.

Dogs are intelligent and brave, and once they've made up their mind, they stick to it. They're quite prepared to go out on a limb for a good cause if necessary, but they don't really like being alone. They're much happier in a group, with close friends or family. What's more, though they're good managers, they're not interested in being in overall charge. They'd much rather help someone else achieve a goal than take all the responsibility themselves.

At work, Dog can be a puzzle to the boss. Though capable of immense effort, and obviously the dedicated type, it's difficult to enthuse the Dog. Promises of pay rises and promotion have little effect. The Dog is just not materialistic or particularly ambitious in the conventional sense. Yet, if a crisis appears, if someone's in trouble or disaster threatens, the Dog is suddenly energised and springs into action. In fact, it's quite difficult to hold Dog back. Dogs will work tirelessly, without rest or thought of reward, until the rescue is achieved.

Bearing this in mind, Dogs would do well to consider a career that offers some kind of humanitarian service. This is their best chance of feeling truly fulfilled and happy at work.

At home, Dogs have a down to earth approach. Home and stability are very important to them. They're not the types to keep moving and trading up, but at the same time, they don't need their home to be a showcase. The Dog residence will be comfortable rather than stylish with the emphasis on practicality. Yet, it will have a warm, inviting atmosphere, and the favoured visitors permitted to join the family there will be certain of a friendly welcome.

It's not easy to get Dog to take a break if there's a cause to be pursued, but when Dogs finally allow themselves to come off-duty, they love to play. They like to be out in the open air or splashing through water, and can discover their competitive streak when it comes to team games.

Best Jobs for Dog

Detective

Solicitor

Teacher

Doctor

Lifeguard

Kennel Manager

Bank Manager

Perfect Partners

Cupid's arrow can strike anywhere at any time, of course, but once the novelty of new romance wears off, some relationships are easier to maintain than others. Here's a guide to the Dog compatibility with other signs.

Dog with Dog

Dogs love company so these two will gravitate to each other and stay there. Both loyal, faithful types, neither need worry the other will stray. They'll appreciate their mutual respect for doing things properly and their shared love of a stable, caring home. This relationship is likely to last and last. The only slight hitch could occur if, over time, the romance dwindles and Dog and Dog become more like good friends than lovers.

Dog with Pig

In the outside world, the Dog and the Pig can get along well together; in fact, Pigs being intelligent creatures can do many of the things dogs can do, so it's not surprising this zodiac pair make a good couple. Good-natured Pig is uncomplicated and fair-minded which suits Dog perfectly. Also, Pig brings out Dog's playful side – which delights Pig who's always keen to have a playmate. A happy relationship involving many restaurants.

Dog with Rat

The Rat and the Dog get along pretty well together. Both strong characters, they respect each other and give each other space when required. But deep down, the Dog is a worrier and gets anxious about unnecessary risks, while Rat just can't help sailing close to the wind if an interesting opportunity presents itself. Long-term, reckless Rat might unintentionally drive Dog to distraction. Only to be considered by Dogs with nerves of steel.

Dog with Ox

These two ought to get along well as they're both sensible, down to earth, loyal, and hardworking, and in tune with each other's basic beliefs. And yet, somehow, they don't. Dog has a playful streak and finds this lacking in Ox, while Ox may be baffled by what seems like pointless silliness in Dog. If they can agree to differ, they could make a relationship work.

Dog with Tiger

While not exactly opposites, these two are different enough to intrigue each other yet similar enough in basic outlook to get on well. Both Tiger and Dog are idealistic and uninterested in material gain yet where Dog can be nervous, Tiger's bold. And where Tiger attracts controversy, Dog will be loyal. This partnership could be lasting and valuable.

Dog with Rabbit

Despite the fact that in the outside world Rabbit could easily end up as Dog's dinner, the astrological pair gets on surprisingly well. Dog appreciates Rabbit's careful, efficient ways and soft voice, while Rabbit admires Dog's energy and good intentions. Dog's lack of interest in the finer points of interior design might try Rabbit's patience, but with a little work, these two could reach an understanding.

Dog with Dragon

Not the easiest of combinations. Down-to-earth Dog can't see what all the fuss is about when it comes to Dragons. Unimpressed by glamour and irritated by what seems to Dog the gullibility of Dragon admirers, Dog can't be bothered to find out more. Dragon meanwhile, is hurt by

Dog's lack of interest. Great determination would be needed to make this work.

Dog with Snake

Some snakes seem to have an almost hypnotic power, and for some reason, Dog is particularly susceptible to these skills. We've heard of snake-charmers, but snakes can be dog-charmers, and without even trying, Snakes can find themselves the recipients of Dog devotion. Since the Dog is strong, loyal, and can be fun, Snake is not averse to this but might, in the end, find it boring.

Dog with Horse

Both good friends of man, these two can make a formidable team. Dog understands the occasional need for solitude while admiring Horse's strength and agility. Horse, meanwhile, senses Dog's loyalty and down to earth nature. Both lovers of the great outdoors and physical activity, they'll never be short of adventures to share. A promising long-term relationship.

Dog with Goat

This is another relationship that could be tricky. Loyal Dog would be quite willing to stand by Goat when practical problems loom but could end up irritated by Goat's inability to learn from previous mistakes and so keeps making them. Goat can't understand why Dog gets so bothered. With care, these two could learn to live together.

Dog with Monkey

Monkey finds Dog intriguing. Monkey senses Dog's strength of character coupled with its playful streak, which fits well with Monkey's love of games. Dog, meanwhile, appreciates Monkey's energy and light-hearted approach. Yet before long, Monkey's disdain for rules will grate on Dog's instinctive love of them. They cannot agree in this area, and it could lead to arguments.

Dog with Rooster

Rooster and Dog are not the best of partners. Dog can be as plain-spoken as Rooster and is not likely to be impressed by overt show. What's more, Dog is often critical, and Rooster can't stand criticism. Rooster, on the other hand, is likely to sense and resent Dog's attitude.

Frustration abounds for both in this relationship. Only for the hopelessly love-struck.

Dog Love 2024 Style

Stand by for some excitement, Dog. Your romantic life is about to get wild. Okay, so you don't often go for wild; you're more the faithful, dependable type. Yet you have to admit, sometimes you look at those crazier zodiac types with their tempestuous love lives and bonkers adventures and feel just the tiniest bit envious.

Well, now it's your turn. Romance is looking for you, and we're not talking conventional. Single Dogs, for some reason, find themselves besieged by unusual, bohemian or just plain outrageous admirers this year. There's something about your calm, wholesome good looks they find incredibly alluring right now.

Maybe they're attracted to the wonderful stability the typical Dog exudes, but as it happens, they're more likely to turn the single Dog's life upside down than the other way around. On the other hand, Dog, you're gonna love the strange perspective.

Attached Dogs could surprise themselves and their partners with a need to get out and about. An unusual restlessness could strike the Dog relationship, and you want to gather up your beloved and go exploring together. There could be more disagreements between you than usual, particularly if your beloved has other plans, but the two of you will enjoy some steamy making-up sessions.

Secrets of Success in 2024

Oddly enough, despite the challenges the Dragon looks likely to bring, this could be one of your most successful years yet, Dog.

The important point to remember is to shake yourself out of any appealing laziness and get stuck in wholeheartedly to whatever job presents itself. If you're typical of your sign, Dog, your family is more important to you than any career. You much prefer to spend time doing nothing in particular with them than climbing the corporate ladder.

Yet, this year, if you pace yourself sensibly, you'll get the opportunity to make great strides in your career *without* neglecting your loved ones. Be sure to take it, and you'll be amazed at how well you do.

The other thing to bear in mind is that 2024 is not the year to take risks with your money. You may be offered an unusual investment. Think very carefully indeed before accepting. Don't raid your savings unless it's absolutely essential.

You're nearly always sensible with your cash, Dog. Keep a cool head and it will grow very nicely this year.

The Dog Year at a Glance

January – A surprisingly fun month. It might be cold outside, but the Dog residence is warm and glowing.

February – You encounter an edgy person in your orbit, at work or in the neighbourhood. Don't argue. Find a way around them.

March – Romance begins to smoulder. There could be more than one amour trying to catch your eye. Decisions, decisions.

April – Someone is trying to take a careless shortcut where they ought to be sticking to the rules. You know how to put things right, but will they let you?

May – It looks like you've fallen for a striking new face. Have they noticed you? They soon will.

June – An old friend has booked a tantalising trip. Can you afford to join them? Can you afford not to?

July – The Dog residence needs a change, or you need a change of residence altogether. Consider the options carefully. You don't have to stay put.

August – A new member is about to join the family. Or could it be a pet? You're going to love them either way.

September – A neighbour gets annoying. You can be tactful when you need to be, Dog. Turn on the charm.

October – Old friends descend. Stand by for long, leisurely meals and hilarious evenings.

November – Young people need your help or at least some mature advice. You're happy to help.

December – You love to entertain, and this Christmas you've got a houseful. Which is just the way you like it.

Lucky colours for 2024: Tangerine, Turquoise, Pine

Lucky numbers for 2024: 1, 5, 7

Three Takeaways

Make time to play.

Put on a friendly smile.

A little luxury is not a sin.
Spoil yourself.

CHAPTER 9: THE PIG

Pig Years

4 February 1935 – 23 January 1936

22 January 1947 – 9 February 1948

8 February 1959 – 27 January 1960

27 January 1971 – 14 February 1972

13 February 1983 – 1 February 1984

31 January 1995 – 18 February 1996

18 February 2007 – 6 February 2008

5 February 2019 – 24 January 2020

23 January 2031 – 10 February 2032

10 February 2043 – 29 January 2044

Natural Element: Water

Will 2024 be a Golden Year for the Pig?

Could it be, Pig, that despite all the hype about the great good fortune of being a Dragon, the unassuming little Pig is actually the luckiest creature in the Chinese zodiac?

You have good cause to wonder. If you're typical of your sign, you've just completed a pretty reasonable 2023 thanks to your friendship with the year's stylish ruler, the Rabbit. Which followed a very promising 2022, courtesy of your other great mucker, the Tiger.

And now 2024 looks like being another agreeable year, thanks to your mate – the Dragon – and its enduring affection for you.

How do you do it, Pig? It seems that despite lacking the obvious glamour of some of the more showy signs, you have the happy knack of rarely antagonising any of them. This means that, in most years, there's a sign in charge that's quite content to let the Pig please itself.

In 2024, it seems quite a few Pigs are still busy with various projects begun the year before. These will gradually pick up speed and accelerate away as the Dragon gets behind them with some much-needed 'oomph'.

Career and business Pigs will then have the opportunity to sign off on the finishing touches and move on to something new. If you fancy a change of job, or even going back to college and retraining, or simply adding another qualification to your CV, this is the year to do it.

It looks as if friends, colleagues and even family members could get themselves involved in your work in 2024. Ventures incorporating team efforts are favoured and likely to prosper. Likewise, Pigs inspired to start new businesses will do well to take on trusted assistants right from the start.

You wouldn't be a Pig, though, if you didn't believe that having a good time is just as important as heading for the top. The good news is that the Dragon recognises Pigs need their R&R and won't penalise you for taking frequent breaks.

2024 will see many Pigs enjoying a whole series of delightful holidays as well as a fair bit of pampering. No need to feel guilty about indulging yourself, Pig, this year… you deserve it.

That's because the only slight drawback of 2024 is that it's a Wood year, and Pigs belong to the Water family.

Wood is very fond of Water because Water nourishes Wood and helps it grow. So, you certainly won't clash with the energy swooshing all around this year. Most Pigs will find they're especially welcome wherever they go. In some circles, you're practically a VIP in 2024, Pig. But it's possible to have too much of a good thing. All that nourishing can be exhausting for a Water creature. In day-to-day life, a strong Wood year can overload a gentle Water sign like the Pig.

Many Pigs could find there's almost more work and opportunity than they can handle, as well as endless demands for their time and support from family and friends. On top of that, while the Pig bank account will swell nicely thanks to that career and business success, so will unavoidable expenses.

Especially sensitive Pigs could find themselves unusually tearful when – at times – the sheer avalanche of EVERYTHING feels overwhelming.

Fortunately, any momentary vulnerability only brings out the Dragon's protective side where Pig is concerned.

This year, it will seem like you've got a Guardian Angel, Pig. Whenever the going gets tough, like a miracle, just the right person will turn up to help you over the difficult patch.

Chances are, any difficulties will be quickly ironed out over a tasty meal, which is just the way Pig likes it.

What it Means to Be a Pig

It takes quite a confident person in the West to announce 'I'm a Pig' to an assembled gathering without embarrassment. Imagine the comments! And if they should happen to be at an event where food is being served, they'd never hear the end of the jokes.

Yet, if you were in China and came out with such a remark, chances are you'd get a very favourable response. You'd certainly not be a figure of fun.

The Chinese zodiac Pig – sometimes known as the Boar – is regarded as a lucky sign. Since flesh and blood pigs tend to have very large litters of baby piglets, they're believed to be a symbol of prosperity and plenty.

And given the Chinese fondness for pork, anyone who owned a pig or two would have been fortunate indeed.

What's more, people born in any Year of the Pig tend to be genuinely amiable types – perhaps the most well-liked of all the 12 signs of the zodiac. Cheerful, friendly, and lacking in ego, they have no enemies. They can fit in anywhere. Nobody objects to a Pig.

Pigs just can't help being kind, sympathetic, and tolerant. Should someone let them down, Pigs will just shrug and insist it wasn't their fault. Pigs tend to get let down over and over again by the same people, but it never occurs to them to bear a grudge. They forgive and forget and move happily along. Friends may scold and warn them not to be a soft touch, but Pigs can't help it. They see no point in conflict.

That's not to say it's impossible to annoy a Pig, just that it takes a great deal to rouse the sweet Pig's nature to anger.

The other refreshing thing about the Pig is that they just want to be happy and have a good time – and they usually do. They find fun in the most unpromising situations, and their enthusiasm is infectious. Soon, everyone else is having fun too.

It's true Pigs enjoy their food – perhaps a little too much – but that's because they are a sensuous sign, appreciating physical pleasures; and it makes them very sexy too.

Shopping is a favourite hobby of many Pigs. They're not greedy; they just love spending money on pretty things simply for the sheer delight of discovering a new treasure and taking it home. This sometimes gets the Pig into trouble because finance isn't a strong point, but such is Pig's charm, they usually get away with it.

Pigs don't tend to be madly ambitious. They have no interest in the rat-race yet they are intelligent and conscientious and can't help being highly effective at work, despite having no ulterior motive or game plan. They often end up in managerial roles. Their sympathetic and conciliatory approach, coupled with their willingness to ask others for advice, goes down well in most organisations and usually leads to promotion. What's more, while avoiding unpleasantness wherever possible, the Pig doesn't like to give up on a task once started, and will invariably find a way to get it done that other signs wouldn't have thought of.

The Pig home reflects the sensuous nature of the Pig. Everything will be comfortable and warm with fabrics and furnishings that feel good as well as look good. Items will be chosen for ease of use rather than style, and there will probably be a great many objects and knick-knacks dotted around, picked up on Pig's shopping expeditions. Pigs quite often excel at cooking, and the Pig kitchen is likely to be crammed with all the latest gadgets and devices for food preparation.

Pigs approve of holidays, of course, and take as many as they can. They're not desperate to tackle extreme sports or go on dangerous expeditions, but they can be adventurous too. They like to be out in the open air, especially if it involves picnics and barbecues but, basically, easy-going Pig's just happy to take a break.

Best Jobs for Pig

Party Planner

Tour Guide

Celebration Cake Maker

Cook

Personal Shopper

Aromatherapist

Restaurant Critic

Perfect Partners

Cupid's arrow can strike anywhere at any time, of course, but once the novelty of new romance wears off, some relationships are easier to maintain than others. Here's a guide to the Pig's compatibility with other signs.

Pig with Pig

When one Pig sets eyes on another Pig, they can't help moving closer for a better look, and should they get talking they probably won't stop. These two understand each other and share so many interests and points of view they seem like a perfect couple. Yet, long-term, they can end up feeling too alike. Pigs rarely argue, yet oddly enough they can find themselves squabbling over trivialities with another Pig. Care needed.

Pig with Rat

It's very easy for Rat to be beguiled by the Pig. Pig's easy-going, sympathetic nature immediately relaxes the Rat. What's more, Pig loves shopping as much as Rat so the two of them could enjoy many happy expeditions together. Conflict could occur through overspending. Pig does not understand Rat's compulsion to bag a bargain. Pig will buy whatever the price and the two could end up arguing over money.

Pig with Ox

Delightful Pig will catch Ox's eye, and since Pig isn't a constant thrill-seeker, the two of them could enjoy many peaceful evenings together, perhaps over a tasty meal. Yet Pig's spendthrift ways – at least in Ox's eyes – could soon prove very annoying as well as illogical to the Ox, while Pig could find Ox's attitude judgemental and upsetting. Not ideal for the long-term.

Pig with Tiger

Carefree Pig will love to bask in Tiger's impressive aura, while Tiger will feel good about protecting this charming but unworldly creature. They enjoy each other's company and Tiger, so focused on lofty matters, will find Pig's compulsive shopping too trivial to worry about. This couple could do well together as long as Pig's fondness for cosy nights in doesn't make Tiger feel trapped.

Pig with Rabbit

Pig is not quite as interested in fine dining as Rabbit, and is happy to scoff a burger as much as a cordon bleu creation, but their shared love of the good things in life makes these two happy companions. Once again, Pig's spending habits might irritate Rabbit, but not too much as

Rabbit is quite willing to splurge on lovely things for the home. A relationship would work well.

Pig with Dragon

While Dragon and Pig might seem to be opposites, the two of them can create a surprisingly contented relationship. Pig is quite happy for Dragon to fly around doing exciting things as long as Pig is not expected to do much more than admire profusely. Dragon appreciates Pig's uncritical support and makes allowances for Pig's lack of stamina. This couple could live in harmony.

Pig with Snake

Pig and Snake don't have a lot to say to each other. Snake can't be bothered with Pig's endless shopping, and Pig is hurt by Snake's snobbish attitude. They both enjoy the good things in life so a luxury fling could briefly be fun – a shared spa break might be a good idea – but in the long-term, this relationship is probably not worth pursuing.

Pig with Horse

Pig and Horse are good companions. Horse is soothed by easy-going Pig and Pig is proud to be seen with such an alluring creature as Horse. They don't have a lot of interests in common, but they don't antagonise each other either. They can jog along amicably for quite a while, but long-term they may find they each want more than the other can provide.

Pig with Goat

Happy-go-lucky Pig and laid-back Goat make a good pair. They hate to stir up trouble and always look for a peaceful solution to any challenge. Ideally, they'd avoid the challenge altogether. They could be very contented together as long as Pig's spending and Goat's inability to deal with finances doesn't get them into trouble.

Pig with Monkey

On the surface, these two might seem an unlikely couple. Yet Pig enjoys Monkey's fun and humour while Monkey is happy to be admired uncritically. What's more, Monkey's inventive mind can solve any difficulties caused by Pig's spending, and since Monkey can't resist a challenge, the opportunity to retrain Pig or at least find a way to obtain purchases cheaper could help the relationship last.

Pig with Rooster

These two might seem an unlikely couple – modest Pig with extrovert Rooster. Yet Pig has no need or wish to crow, and can see the vulnerable character that lurks beneath Rooster's fine feathers. While Rooster responds to Pig's kindness and undemanding nature. As long as Rooster doesn't get bored, this can be a contented relationship.

Pig with Dog

In the outside world, the dog and the pig can get along well together; in fact, pigs, being intelligent creatures, can do many of the things dogs can do, so it's not surprising this zodiac pair make a good couple. Good-natured Pig is uncomplicated and fair-minded which suits Dog perfectly. Also, Pig brings out Dog's playful side – which delights Pig who's always keen to have a playmate. A happy relationship involving many restaurants.

Pig Love 2024 Style

You're such a sensuous, sexy sign, Pig, it's no wonder you're popular and – in 2024 – you become a bit of a superstar. Single Pigs will find their sunny personalities are suddenly essential ingredients at every gathering. It has something to do with the delightful Pig attitude: cheerful and uncritical, combined with voluptuous good looks and a happy smile. Who could resist the total Pig package?

As usual, single Pigs will have their choice of admirers, but this year more than one of them could get a bit over the top. Devotion is in danger of turning into obsession, which is very difficult for the Pig to understand.

Kindly Pigs always want their friends to avoid disappointment, but disentangling gently from an unwanted love might prove challenging this year. Consider calling in a pal to help.

Attached Pigs are in the mood for love, but harmony at home could be hampered by interruptions. Unexpected visitors, friends in need of sympathy, neighbours who've lost their keys, stray dogs seeking shelter – somehow, they all end up at the Pig front door. Knowing you, Pig, you'll welcome them in, break out the snacks, and end up having an uproarious evening. Romance might have to wait, but fun's fun.

Secrets of Success in 2024

The good news, Pig, is that this year, the best way for you to proceed is to make sure you don't try too hard.

Yes, you did read that right! If you're typical of your sign, chances are you can hardly believe it. This is not the kind of advice you're used to. Usually, you're required to do the exact opposite.

The difference this year, Pig, is that the combination of the generous, friendly Dragon with the expansive energy of Wood, means that success, opportunity and cash come fairly easily to you. Slaving away is not necessary. That's not an excuse for a lie-in every day of the week, of course. Laziness is not advisable, either. Just make sure you attend to important tasks in a sensible, responsible manner. Do what you need to do, but no more.

There's more danger of you burning out right now if you overload yourself, than of you blowing your chances because you failed to put in extra hours.

The secret this year, Pig, is to pace yourself, accept any help offered, organise plenty of fun trips, and don't overdo it with the eating and drinking!

The Pig Year at a Glance

January – The holidays are a fading memory, but you keep the mood high with some retro partying.

February – A new face in the neighbourhood attracts much attention. Time you introduced yourself.

March – Workplace romance is blossoming. Could this be something special or just a diversion?

April – Promotion beckons at work, but do you want the extra responsibility? Talk things over with a friend.

May – Jealous eyes are watching. Your success upsets a colleague. Can't be helped, Pig.

June – A lively friend suggests a break. The more the merrier, Pig.

July – Romance is getting heavy. Should you cool things down or go with the flow? Follow your instincts.

August – Picnics and barbie time Chez Pig. Huge amounts of cooking going on. Enjoy.

September – Your career is ticking over nicely. There's plenty to do, and you're tempted to stay late. Don't overdo it.

October – A foodie friend suggests a restaurant tour. There are new eateries to sample. It's rude not to agree.

November – Festive decorations going up all over town. You love this time of year. Shopping, shopping, shopping. Pig bliss.

December – Santa's elves were probably zodiac Pigs. You can't wait for the big day. Festive fun all round.

Lucky colours for 2024: Silver, Green, Scarlet

Lucky numbers for 2024: 2, 5, 7

Three Takeaways

Lock up your credit cards.

Remember your five a day.

Think bargain, not full price.

CHAPTER 10: THE RAT

Rat Years

5 February 1924 – 24 January 1925

24 January 1936 – 10 February 1937

10 February 1948 – 28 January 1949

28 January 1960 – 14 February 1961

15 February 1972 – 2 February 1973

2 February 1984 – 19 February 1985

19 February 1996 – 7 February 1997

7 February 2008 – 25 January 2009

25 January 2020 – 11 February 2021

11 February 2032 – 30 January 2033

30 January 2044 – 16 February 2045

Natural Element: Water

Will 2024 be a Golden Year for the Rat?

Congratulations, Rat. Along with your very good mate, the Monkey, you've just become joint winner of the Most Favoured Sign of 2024 Award.

Okay, so you'd probably like some kind of medal, or at least a nice glossy badge (preferably gold, preferably 24-carat) to wear. Sorry, it's not on offer. But what you do get is worth its weight in precious metal, and knowing you, by the year's end, you'll probably have stashed an impressive haul of the shiny stuff anyway.

You leave 2023 a little more rested and relaxed than you began it, if you're typical of your sign, Rat, and also rather admired in some quarters. But, whisper it softly, you're probably also, ever so slightly bored.

While the refined Rabbit of 2023 was a refreshing interlude, ultimately it didn't provide enough of a challenge for the wily Rat. You needed the downtime to reboot and recharge, but now you're bristling with suppressed energy.

This is why the exuberant Dragon's entrance is so perfect for you. As well as the fact that you and the Dragon are such great mates, the huge surge of power that accompanies the Dragon – so overwhelming for more delicate signs – is like plugging into the mains for a robust rodent like you.

Suddenly, the typical Rat is right back on form. Zooming around, chatting non-stop, examining every opportunity, inspecting every angle, taking on ten things at once if at all possible.

Entrepreneurial Rats – which is basically all of you, even if you've got a day job – are in for a treat. This year, you're being urged to scent out every deal, track down every bargain, and launch those projects you've had on the back burner since lockdown.

Bold Rats that think big will be rewarded. New businesses will take off, new roles will be offered at work, and opportunities to present Rat ideas in front of an audience will materialise. If you ever fancied going into politics, showbusiness, or inspirational speaking, Rat, this could be your big chance. In 2024, you could certainly make a name for yourself.

Employed Rats will be busier than ever and flavour of the month at work, yet their biggest success could come through turning a hobby into cash. Whether it's discovering a Ming vase at a car boot sale, launching those ancient threads at the back of the wardrobe into a vintage emporium, or inventing a new cocktail, a Rat enthusiasm or side hustle could suddenly morph into big business.

The cash will come rolling in, of course, Rat, and like the shrewd rodent you are, you'll probably stash it away in the highest interest account you can find. The Rat coffers will be growing very fast this year.

Yet no year would go by without challenges, and despite your favoured position, Rat, you're bound to have some ups and downs. This is partly due to the fact that, like your cosmic cousin the Pig, you're a Water creature and this is a Wood year.

At first glance, this is a good thing. The two elements are complementary to each other. Wood enjoys Water because Water helps Wood grow, and Water is quite happy to assist Wood. In fact, like a proud parent, Water is usually pleased with Wood's progress, but at the same time, there are drawbacks. All that nourishing can be exhausting. What's more, amongst other things, Water represents emotions and Wood energy amplifies what it finds.

So, in a Wood year, Rats can find themselves besieged with needy relatives and friends, or argumentative workmates wanting Rat to referee. In turn, business associates and colleagues could be prone to overreacting to the slightest setback – requiring urgent injections of Rat diplomacy to restore calm.

If you're typical of your sign, Rat, you're going to be busy, busy, busy, but despite your protests, that's exactly what you love. And somehow, you'll still find time to let that adoring family of yours drag you off for a splendid holiday.

What it Means to Be a Rat

It doesn't sound so good does it, to call yourself a Rat? In fact, it may seem strange to start the astrological cycle with such a controversial creature as the unwelcome rodent. Here in the West, we haven't a good word to say about them. We talk of 'plagues' of rats; they 'infest' dirty, derelict places; they hang around dustbins.

They're associated with disease, rubbish, and sewers, and if a rat should be spied near our homes, we'd be straight on the phone to pest control. They make us shudder. Describe a person as 'a rat', and you're certainly not paying them a compliment.

Yet, the Chinese view things differently. When they think of the zodiac Rat, they're thinking not of the flea-ridden rodent with the disconcerting long, hairless tail. They're imagining a certain energy, certain admirable qualities they associate with the creature. Rats, after all, are a very successful species. They are great survivors; they're quick, intelligent, tenacious, and they seem to thrive almost anywhere, under any conditions. All excellent qualities to be commended, if you found them in a human.

So, far from being an unfortunate sign, being born in the year of the Rat is regarded as a good omen.

Rats possess great charm and elegance. They're chatty, intelligent, and make friends easily. At parties, people seem drawn to them. There's something about their genuine enjoyment of being surrounded by new faces that makes them easy to get along with. Yet, they value old friends too, will make an effort to stay in touch, and a friendship with a rat is likely to last a lifetime.

Both male and female rats always look good. They believe that outward appearances are important. Instinctively, they understand that you only get one chance to make a first impression, so they take care never to be caught off-guard looking a mess.

This happy knack is easier for them than most because they love shopping and are Olympic-standard bargain hunters. They can't resist a sale and if it's a designer outlet, so much the better. Their homes are usually equally smart for the same reason. Rats have innate good taste and are as thrilled with finding a stylish chair, or piece of artwork at half price, as they are a pair of shoes.

They enjoy spending money and the challenge of hunting down the best deal; and because they're also successful at work, they tend to have plenty of cash to splurge. Yet, despite this, Rats can often be viewed as a bit stingy. They're not mean, it's just that Rats' strong survival instincts lead them to prioritise themselves and their family when it comes to allocating their resources. Within their families, Rats are extremely generous.

Rats also enjoy the finer things in life. They prefer not to get their hands dirty if at all possible and are experts at getting other people to do mundane tasks for them. They like pampering and luxury and lavish holidays. Yet, being supremely adaptable, they will happily embark on a backpacking trip if it takes them where they want to go and there's no other option. They're adventurous, and hate to be bored, so they're prepared to take a calculated risk if some place or person catches their eye.

Yet, this willingness to take a risk combined with the love of a bargain can occasionally get them into trouble, despite their super-sensitive survival instincts. Rats, particularly male Rats, have to guard against the urge to gamble. The combination of the prospect of winning easy money, the excitement of the element of chance, and the challenge of pitting their wits against the odds can prove irresistible. What starts as a mild flirtation for fun can end up as quite a problem.

The same could be said for suspect 'get-rich-quick' schemes. Though clever and sceptical enough to see through them, Rats are so thrilled by the idea of an easy gain, the temptation to cast doubts aside, against their better judgement, can be overwhelming.

But if any sign can get away with such unwise habits, it's probably the Rat. Rats are good at making money and handling money. They're also masters at spotting an escape route and scuttling away down it if the going gets too tough. Underneath that gregarious bonhomie, there's a shrewd, observant brain that misses nothing. Rats have very sharp eyes and are highly observant even when they don't appear to be taking any notice. They are also very ambitious, though they tend to keep it quiet. Dazzled by their genuine charm and witty conversation, people often fail to see that most moves Rats make are taking them methodically to the top. It's no accident they call it 'the rat race'.

Best Jobs for Rats in 2024

Motivational Speaker

Antiques Dealer

Electric Car Salesperson

Estate Agent

Stock Broker

Perfect Partners 2024

Cupid's arrow can strike anywhere at any time, of course, but once the novelty of new romance wears off, some relationships are easier to maintain than others. Here's a guide to the Rat's compatibility with other signs.

Rat with Rat

These two are certainly on the same wavelength and share many interests. When their eyes first meet, passionate sparks may fly. This relationship could work very well, though over time the competitive and ambitious nature of both partners could see them pulling in different directions. What's more, if one should succumb to a weakness for gambling or risky business ventures while the other does not, it will end in tears.

Rat with Ox

Oddly enough, this combination can be surprisingly successful. Frenetic Rat and calm Ox may seem to be opposites but, in fact, Rat can find Ox's laid-back approach strangely soothing. Ox is not interested in competing with Rat and will put up with Rat's scurrying after new schemes with patience. As long as Rat doesn't get bored and has enough excitement in other areas of life, this relationship could be very contented.

Rat with Tiger

The magnificent Tiger will always catch Rat's eye because Rat loves beautiful things, but Tiger's natural element is Wood and Rat's is Water which means that Tiger wears Rat out. What's more, Tiger's not interested in Rat's latest bargain, and Rat doesn't share Tiger's passion for changing the world, yet the attraction is strong. If Rat makes an effort to step back and not get in Tiger's way, they could reach a good understanding.

Rat with Rabbit

Rat finds Rabbit intriguing. Here is an attractive, stylish creature that doesn't feel the need to be pushy or take centre stage yet somehow manages to be at the heart of things. The Rat wants to find out more, while Rabbit is flattered and entertained by witty Rat's attention. These two respect each other but, over the long-term, Rat could be too overpowering.

Rat with Dragon

This couple is usually regarded as a very good match. They have much in common being action-loving, excitement-seeking personalities who hate to be bored. It takes a lot to dazzle Rat, but the Dragon's glamorous aura proves irresistible, while Dragon loves to be admired, so each enjoys being with the other. There could be the odd power struggle as these two are both strong characters, but the magnetism is so powerful they usually kiss and make up.

Rat with Snake

The Snake shares Rat's good taste and being elegant, sophisticated, and smart will delight Rat at first sight. These two get on very well on an intellectual level but perhaps are better as good friends rather than long-term partners. The Snake's love of basking in the sun for hours strikes Rat as lazy and dull, while Rat's need to rush around doing deals and meeting people seems pointless and wearying to the Snake.

Rat with Horse

Rat and Horse both fizz with energy and they love action and looking good, yet this is not seen as an ideal partnership. Nothing's impossible, of course, but these two will have to work hard to find harmony. The Rat will admire Horse's enthusiasm and cheerful approach but become impatient to discover Horse can also be fiery and emotional. Horse, on the other hand, can find Rat's risk-taking behaviour extremely worrying.

Rat with Goat

The Rat is charmed by carefree Goat and fascinated by its artistic talent and happy knack of living in the present. Easy-going Goat tends to like everyone so is perfectly content to enjoy Rat's company. These two can get along fine, yet they don't really understand each other deep down. Long-term, the Rat may find Goat's lack of interest in the practical side of life, such as finances and bills, irritating.

Rat with Monkey

Unlikely as it might appear, mischievous Monkey and the clever Rat make a good partnership. Their quick minds, sociable natures, and love of novelty ensure that they're never bored together. True, Rat might sometimes feel Monkey is too inclined to skim over the surface of things and could do with being more serious at times, but Monkey's ingenuity and audaciousness always save the day. Both can have a weakness for gambling though, so need to take care.

Rat with Rooster

The first thing Rat notices about the Rooster is its beautiful plumage, but this a relationship which is unlikely to get much further than initial admiration. Rooster's direct and frank approach can strike the Rat as tactless, while the Rooster can't understand why Rat has to make life so convoluted and complicated. Then again, Rooster's natural confidence and aplomb can come across as bragging to the Rat. These two have to be very determined to make a partnership work.

Rat with Dog

The Rat and the Dog get along pretty well together. Both are strong characters, and they respect each other and give each other space when required. But deep down, the Dog is a worrier and gets anxious about unnecessary risks, while Rat just can't help sailing close to the wind if an interesting opportunity presents itself. Long-term, reckless Rat might unintentionally drive Dog to distraction. Only to be considered by Dogs with nerves of steel.

Rat with Pig

It's very easy for Rat to be beguiled by the Pig. Pig's easy-going, sympathetic nature immediately relaxes the Rat. What's more, Pig loves shopping as much as Rat so the two of them could enjoy many happy expeditions together. Conflict could occur through overspending. Pig does not understand Rat's compulsion to bag a bargain, while Rat can't fathom why Pig is prepared to pay whatever's asked, but with compromise on both sides this could work well.

Rat Love 2024 Style

Put the Rat in a social setting, and all you have to do is stand back and watch a master at work. Rat can work a room like Picasso could paint a picture. The rodent, charming a crowd, makes it look effortless and completely natural. Other signs try the same thing and just end up looking silly.

So, it's no surprise the single Rat usually leaves any event with the partner of their choice on their arm. If their twinkly good looks don't work sufficient magic, their witty repartee will seal the deal.

Yet, the typical Rat doesn't abuse their rodent advantage. In fact, you can be quite picky, Rat. Single or attached, Rat is quite happy to flirt outrageously all night but sashay off home alone rather than settle for the wrong partner. When it comes to serious romance, Rat has high standards.

So, this looks like being a vintage year for fantastic flirtations, Rat. Both single and attached Rats are set to have a blast. Single Rats might not find their soul mate, but they'll have enormous fun looking.

Attached Rats, on the other hand, could encounter some friction on the home front if their beloved doesn't appreciate all that unnecessary flirting. Jealousy could cause some emotional scenes. It's no good protesting that a little light banter never hurt anyone, Rat. Reserve some of that sparkling wit for your loved one; make a big fuss of them and peace will be restored.

Secrets of Success in 2024

You hardly need telling to 'go for it', Rat. This is your year for making it big, and you know it.

What's more, you understand – better than most – that the one thing that annoys the Dragon is ignoring Dragon generosity and opportunities. So, you'll keep those sharp eyes alert for every prospect, no matter how unlikely. You're determined not to miss a thing.

As usual though, Rat, you need to curb your tendency to leap onto any suggestion that promises a short-cut. You're brilliant at cutting corners and teasing out the quickest and cheapest way to your goals – there was a reason you came first in that Imperial race all those years ago, after all.

Yet, despite that, you're in such a hurry, you often fail to properly examine proposals put to you by others. You assume they know what they're talking about because they sound so plausible.

The trouble is, some are not as clever as you, Rat, and others are not as honest. Slow down and take the time to check all the details before committing any rodent cash.

Then there's burn out. Your energy is legendary, Rat. Why do one thing when you can manage six is your philosophy. But Dragon energy is even more powerful than yours, Rat, and the Wood element so strong it can drain a Water creature like you. Take care to pace yourself, timetable frequent entertaining but relaxing breaks and your prospects for 2024 are phenomenal.

The Rat Year at a Glance

January – Things are beginning to seem a bit dull. You're searching around for something new. Keep looking – it's out there.

February – A bargain materialises. There could be an obstacle in your path, but don't give up… you'll find a way around it.

March – A new face at work is intrigued by you. You're only too happy to discuss your talents.

April – The boss reckons you're onto something special, Rat. Time to hint about a pay rise?

May – A slippery type has an interesting proposition. Is everything as it seems, though? Don't rush in.

June – Business opportunities abound, but temperaments could clash. Much patience is required.

July – A quirky face cruises by and your interest is captured. Not your usual type, but variety is the spice of life!

August – A naughty friend leads you astray. Quite nice to be naughty at times, though. You usually get away with it, Rat.

September – Career prospects are looking good. Whether it's your own business or promotion at work, expect some good news soon.

October – A reunion is on the cards. You're very busy, but make the time. You'll regret it if you pass.

November – You're in charge, Rat. At home or at work, you must take over the reins suddenly. You quite enjoy being the boss.

December – It's party time at the rodent residence, and it looks like you'll be partying all month. Try not to overdo it, Rat.

Lucky colours for 2024: Emerald, Blue and Silver

Lucky numbers for 2024: 4, 8

Three Takeaways

Ration phone time.

Consider yoga classes – then attend.

Be alert to scams.

CHAPTER 11: THE OX

Ox Years

25 January 1925 – 12 February 1926
11 February 1937 – 30 January 1938
29 January 1949 – 16 February 1950
15 February 1961 – 4 February 1962
3 February 1973 – 22 January 1974
20 February 1985 – 8 February 1986
8 February 1997 – 27 January 1998
26 January 2009 – 13 February 2010
12 February 2021 – 31 January 2022
31 January 2033 – 18 February 2034
17 February 2045 – 5 February 2046
Natural Element: Water

Will 2024 be a Golden year for the Ox?

The good news, Ox, is that 2024 is not going to be a repeat of 2022. The scary old Tiger of two years ago is long gone and not due back for another decade.

The not quite such good news is that the Dragon of 2024 is another big, demanding, over-the-top kind of character. Similar to the formidable Tiger, but different in all sorts of ways beneficial to an intelligent yet sensitive Ox such as yourself.

Last year, if you were typical of your sign, things went pretty well. The Ox and the Rabbit ruler of the year get on beautifully, so the Oxen path was smoothed wherever possible in all directions, but in a gentle, steady manner.

This means that many an Ox enters 2024 with their finances in a healthier state than quite a few of their cosmic cousins, and with some noticeable progress in career matters, too.

Don't worry Ox. All this will continue. It's just that Dragon energy is more forceful than Rabbit's. The tempo of your life is about to increase, the volume whooshes up a notch or three, and you'll be expected to keep pace.

While not being quite besties, you and the Dragon respect each other. The Dragon admires your sincere work ethic and intends to help you make even more progress. Dragon also reckons you haven't received the recognition you deserve and wishes to put this right.

Dragon 'assistance' could arrive as a deluge of extra work, job offers or, in the case of self-employed or business Oxen, a stream of eager new clients. An increase in profits and opportunity for finance is also likely to accompany this good fortune. It's all designed to help you expand your career or business, Ox.

You'll be encouraged to take on more staff, or persuade the boss to hire you some helpers. You may also be given the chance to increase your knowledge of some important and potentially lucrative aspect of your profession.

And don't be surprised if you find yourself unexpectedly put up for some kind of award. Even if you don't want to be. You're going to get noticed, Ox – like it or not – so take that horrified look off your face.

If all this sounds worryingly like the Tiger approach to the year, keep calm. Dragon energy is not so brash and bruising. The Dragon is less impatient than the Tiger where you're concerned and more forgiving. You won't be punished should you fall behind.

Like the Rabbit, the Dragon of 2024 belongs to the Wood family of creatures, while the Ox is from the Water tribe. Wood folk like the company of Water types since Wood needs Water to grow. So, there's no antagonism between you; it's just that Water creatures like the Ox can find Wood animal years literally draining, though they can't quite put their finger on why.

And it's not just the Dragon wafting Wood in your direction, Ox. The element for the whole year happens to be Wood, too. So, we have Wood on Wood, magnifying the effect.

The result is likely to be that every aspect of the Ox life feels as if it's expanding in all directions at a dizzying rate. Career, your social circle, even the Ox home – all are affected. The old, familiar (if rather tight) boundaries are melting and re-erecting further away. So much so that many Oxen will need to consider moving to larger premises in 2024 or building an extension.

The great thing about 2024, though, is that the typical Ox will be able to spend far more time outdoors. This is particularly beneficial for you, Ox, because being in the open air, especially in natural surroundings, will restore any vitality depleted by an excess of Wood energy. Despite being surrounded by growing things that could prove tiring to a Water creature, the Ox thrives in the green.

Oxen involved in forestry, agriculture, horticulture, festivals or outdoor businesses of any kind will do exceptionally well. They'll also find themselves having to make more site visits than usual.

At home, the typical Ox will be inspired to round up family and friends for impromptu picnics, country breaks, sports events, festivals, parties in the garden – you name it. If it's fun in the sun, the Ox will be there. Stand by also, Ox, to develop a sudden interest in tending an allotment, going camping, or maybe experimenting with metal detecting.

There's a lot for you to like about 2024, Ox. You could even end up making a fortune. So, get out there and make the most of it!

What it Means to Be an Ox

Okay, so hands up everyone who's secretly disappointed to be an astrological Ox?

Sounds a bit bovine and boring, doesn't it? The Ox might lack the glamour of the Tiger or the Dragon. It can't even boast the intriguing notoriety of a sign like the Rat or the Snake. In fact, here in the West, we may not even be entirely sure what an Ox looks like. Some sort of large cow, perhaps?

So, at first sight, you might be excused for thinking the Ox was dull. Yet, in China, that wasn't the perception at all. There was a very good reason the Ox was so highly placed – at number two – on the zodiac wheel.

The animal was revered as essential to country life. So precious, it was regarded as a gift from the Gods. So special, in fact, it's said that in the past the Chinese didn't eat beef. They couldn't possibly disrespect such an important beast by serving it up for dinner.

So, while the Ox may not seem as exciting as some of the other celestial animals, the sign of the Ox is respected and appreciated.

What the Chinese valued was the phenomenal strength and endurance of the Ox. Get an Ox moving, and it will plod on mile after mile, covering huge distances with apparent ease and without complaint. Without the work of the Ox, many a family would have gone hungry.

People born in the year of the zodiac Ox are believed to be blessed with similar qualities. For this reason, though unflashy and quietly spoken, they often end up being extremely successful in whatever they undertake – from their career to their favourite hobby, or creating a harmonious family that blossoms.

Oxen have a wonderful knack of planning a sensible, logical course to wherever they want to go and then following it, relentlessly, step by step until they get there, no matter what obstacles they encounter en-route. Oxen find it rather puzzling that other people can't seem to adopt the same simple approach. They don't understand why some signs give up before reaching their goal. Why do they waste their time chopping and changing and getting nowhere, wonders the Ox.

Ox patience is legendary. They may not be quick, or nimble, but they realise that slow, steady, consistent effort achieves far more in the long run. And the Ox is only interested in the long haul. At heart, the Ox is serious-minded, and though they enjoy a joke as much as anyone else, they regard frivolity as a pleasant diversion, not an end in itself.

Ox people are usually good-looking in a healthy, wholesome way, but they're not impressed by flashy, passing whims and fashions. Superficial gloss has no appeal. The Ox woman is unlikely to be found rocking extreme, designer clothes or wafting fingers iridescent with the latest nail polish.

Ox tastes tend to be classic and practical. They are instinctively private and hate to draw attention to themselves, yet the Ox is one of the nicest signs. Genuinely honest, kind, and sincere, Ox is ready to help anyone in trouble, happily pitching in to lend a hand without expecting anything in return. Yet, since Ox tends to speak only when they have something to say, other signs can find them difficult to get to know. It's worthwhile making the effort because the Ox will be a loyal friend forever.

What's more, when they do have something to say, Ox views can be surprisingly frank. Just because they are patient and kind, it doesn't mean they can be pushed around. The Ox is self-reliant and makes up its own mind; it's not swayed by the opinions of others. What's more, they can be very stubborn. When the Ox finally makes a decision, it sees no reason to change it.

Ox people are not materialistic. They work hard because the task interests them, or because they can see it needs to be done, and they will keep going until the project is complete. They are the true craftsmen of the zodiac, excelling in working with their hands and they can be unexpectedly artistic and innovative when the occasion demands. As a result, money can accumulate and Ox is not averse to spending it on some creature comforts. The Ox home will be warm and styled for comfort and practicality rather than cutting-edge design. If there's no space for a garden, it's likely to be filled with houseplants too, because Ox has green fingers and needs to see nature close at hand.

Travel and holidays are not top of the Ox agenda; they enjoy their work and their home and are not forever itching to get away. Unlike many signs, they cope with routine very well. And for all their modesty and quiet diligence, there is always something impressive about the Ox. Other signs sense the latent strength and power that lies just below the surface and tend not to impose too much. This is just as well because though the Ox may appear calm, placid, and slow to anger, when they do finally lose their temper, it can be terrifying. What's more, the Ox will never forget an insult and can bear a grudge for years. Ox doesn't stay mad – they get even.

Best Jobs for Ox 2024

Florist

Solicitor

Farmer

Dog Breeder

Teacher

Electrician

Potter

Perfect Partners

Cupid's arrow can strike anywhere at any time, of course, but once the novelty of new romance wears off, some relationships are easier to maintain than others. Here's a guide to the Ox's compatibility with other signs.

Ox with Ox

These two could be very happy together, as long as one of them plucks up the courage to admit they're interested. Sloppy, sentimental romance is not their style and they both share this view so there'll be no misunderstandings around Valentine's Day. They know that still waters run deep and they can enjoy great contentment without showy declarations of love.

Ox with Tiger

Not an easy match. Ox and Tiger could be on different planets. Fiery Tiger doesn't frighten Ox and Tiger may admire Ox's strong, good looks and sincere nature but they both need different things from life. Tiger wants to dash about changing the world for the better, while Ox reckons you get more done by buckling down where you happen to be and attending to the details. Clashes could abound.

Ox with Rabbit

Ox finds Rabbit rather cute and appealing. Whether male or female there's something about Rabbit's inner fluffiness that brings out Ox's highly developed protective instincts. Rabbit meanwhile loves the Ox's reassuring presence and the sense of security Ox provides. These two could get on very well together as long as refined Rabbit can overlook Ox's occasional down-to-earth – Rabbit might say 'coarse' - observations.

Ox with Dragon

Chalk and cheese though this pair may appear to be there's a certain fascination between them. Ox may not approve of Dragon's showy manner but recognises Dragon's good intentions, while Dragon admires Ox's strength of character and gift for completing tasks. If each could find a way to tolerate the other's wildly different lifestyles, they might be good for each other, but long term, Dragon's hectic pace might wear even the Ox's legendary stamina.

Ox with Snake

Like Ox, the Snake is quietly ambitious and not given to racing around unless it's absolutely necessary. Ox, on the other hand, respects Snake's clever brain and understated elegance. These two could quickly discover how beneficial an alliance between them would be. They're both happy to give the other space when required but also step in with support when needed. This could be a very successful match.

Ox with Horse

Long ago, on many Western farms, Ox was replaced by the Horse and it may be that Ox has never forgotten and never forgiven. At any rate, these two, despite both being big, strong animals, are not usually friends. Horse is too flighty and frivolous to interest Ox for long, while Ox's methodical, careful ways will irritate the Horse. Best not to go there.

Ox with Goat

Though these two share artistic natures even if in the case of the Ox, they're well hidden, deep down, they don't 'get' one another. Ox may be beguiled at first by Goat's friendly, easy-going manner but then disappointed to discover Goat seems to find everyone equally delightful, even those who're plainly unworthy. Goat, on the other hand, can't understand why Ox won't lighten up more. This relationship would require a lot of effort and compromise.

Ox with Monkey

The naughty Monkey scandalises Ox, but in such an amusing way that Ox can't help laughing. Monkey, on the other hand, is equally amused to find an audience so easy to shock. This unlikely pair enjoy each other's company and get on surprisingly well. Yet, right from the start, it's probably obvious to both that a long term relationship couldn't last. A fun flirtation, though, could be a terrific tonic for them both.

Ox with Rooster

For all its bravado and showing off, the Rooster is a down-to-earth type, drawn to security and accumulating the good things in life – requirements that Ox understands very well and can supply effortlessly. What's more, Ox can't help but admire Rooster's fine feathers and skill at communicating in a crowd – attributes Ox doesn't have and is unlikely to acquire. These two could enjoy a very good partnership.

Ox with Dog

These two ought to get along well as they're both sensible, down to earth, loyal and hardworking and in tune with each other's basic beliefs. And yet, somehow, they don't. Dog has a playful streak and finds this lacking in Ox, while Ox may be baffled by what seems like pointless silliness in Dog. If they can agree to differ, they could make a relationship work.

Ox with Pig

Delightful Pig will catch Ox's eye, and since Pig isn't a constant thrill-seeker, the two of them could enjoy many peaceful evenings together, perhaps over a tasty meal. Yet Pig's spendthrift ways – at least in Ox's eyes, could soon prove very annoying as well as illogical to the Ox, while Pig could find Ox's attitude judgemental and upsetting. Not ideal for the long term.

Ox with Rat

Oddly enough, this combination can be surprisingly successful. Frenetic Rat and calm Ox may seem to be opposites, but in fact Rat can find Ox's laid-back approach strangely soothing. Ox is not interested in competing with Rat and will patiently put up with Rat's scurrying after new schemes. As long as Rat doesn't get bored and generates enough excitement in other areas of life, this relationship could be very contented.

Ox Love 2024 Style

The Ox would have you believe they don't go in for online dating, can't be faffed with messing about with their hair, or fussing over their clothes in case they bump into someone alluring. All that shallow stuff that so bafflingly preoccupies other signs.

You take the Ox as you find them, they insist, and if you don't like what you see, your loss.

Yet, somehow, the Ox always manages to impress while protesting all the time it's the last thing on their mind. And this year is no exception. In fact, this year, the Ox is set to dazzle.

Single Oxen could find themselves suddenly thrust – bewildered and blinking – into the spotlight, with other signs clamouring for attention. The more you try to wriggle away from the crowd, the more intriguingly attractive you become, Ox. There's something about your strong, understated good looks and natural grace that's immensely appealing. You're refreshingly authentic, Ox (that's what it is!), and that's a rare quality these days.

No doubt about it, romance is on fire for the single Ox. You can't remember a time you were more popular. You may not quite understand what's happened, Ox, but no point in fighting it. Just relax and enjoy.

The attached Ox has a delightful year, too. You and your partner are both so busy with exciting developments at work, you long for cosy nights at home, winding down together by the fire with a bottle of your favourite fizz and a takeaway.

Secrets of Success in 2024

The typical Ox begins the year in the happy position of having the accounts up to date, important paperwork safely filed, diary properly organised, and a great many lists pinned up everywhere, quite possibly in alphabetical order. If not on top of absolutely everything, most Oxen have made a very good start.

Unfortunately, it could all go severely downhill from here, Ox, if you don't prepare to improvise. Very soon, so many tasks, so much work, so many queries, rearrangements and unexpected events are likely to hit you; your lists will disintegrate, the files collapse, and you could suffer a meltdown.

The trouble is, Ox, you have your systems and you like to stick to them. They're efficient, tried and tested. You know they work. They've served you well in the past. All this is true, it's just that the Dragon demands innovation, creative thinking, and bold experiments, while the Wood energy insists on expansion.

The only way you're going to cope with the torrent of opportunities and requests coming your way, Ox, is to dump your set routines and make it up as you go along. Flexibility is the key to success in 2024 – along with a willingness to try a new approach.

You must admit you can be a tad stubborn on occasion, Ox, so you won't appreciate being obliged to make changes. Yet, if you manage to locate your inner elasticity and dare to act a little audaciously, you'll be amazed by the brilliance of your prospects.

The Ox Year at a Glance

January – A peaceful month. A sense of calm settles over the workplace and you can get a lot done.

February – Someone in your orbit gets bossy. They think they're the boss, but they're not. Be subtle (you can do subtle, Ox), but quietly put them in their place.

March – It looks like you've got a fan. Someone has quite a crush. Do you feel the same way? Follow your instincts.

April – Accolades are coming your way, Ox. You're not sure you've done enough to deserve all this, but no need to protest.

May – A helpful colleague wants to come to your assistance, Ox? It would be rude not to accept. This could be the start of something interesting.

June – Suddenly, a rival appears on the scene, at work or in your love life. Don't stand for it, Ox. This is not the time for modesty.

July – Friends or relatives have had too much sun. Well, so it seems to you. They're being irresponsible, so can you make them see sense? Unlikely, but you try.

August – A partner suggests taking the whole month off. Impossible, of course, but you like the idea. Can you extend your holiday?

September – Romance is getting hot. Invitations are flowing in, and you need to choose. One that you're inclined to turn down could lead to love.

October – Someone at work is even more respectful of the regulations than you, Ox. They could be annoying. Charm them with your superior knowledge.

November – An admirer gives you a gift, but it looks expensive. Too expensive. Should you accept? Think carefully.

December – Relatives want you at theirs for the festivities. It could be good to relax. Put your feet up and enjoy.

Lucky colours for 2024: Navy blue, Silver, Orange

Lucky numbers for 2024: 2, 8, 9

Three Takeaways

Turn on the charm.

Unleash your wild side.

Get out and make new friends.

CHAPTER 12: THE TIGER

Tiger Years

13 February 1926 – 1 February 1927

31 January 1938 – 18 February 1939

17 February 1950 – 5 February 1951

5 February 1962 – 24 January 1963

23 January 1974 – 10 February 1975

9 February 1986 – 28 January 1987

28 January 1998 – 5 February 1999

14 February 2010 – 2 February 2011

1 February 2022 – 21 January 2023

19 February 2034 – 7 February 2035

6 February 2046 – 25 January 2047

Natural Element: Wood

Will 2024 be a Golden Year for the Tiger?

Well, Tiger, excellent news. Kinda. 2024 looks like being an explosive year! While some of your zodiac cousins might find such an outlook daunting, the mighty Tiger relishes the prospect.

At last, a year worthy of the Tiger's formidable skills. 2024 provides you with a vast stage on which to perform magnificently. If you're typical of your sign, you can hardly wait.

There are several reasons for this. For a start, you and the Dragon ruler of the year are the most impressive, most dominant creatures in the zodiac. You both expect to be the boss. You're both natural leaders and neither of you takes orders from anyone. So, whichever of you happens to be in charge, sparks are certain to fly with the other. Clashes abound.

You and the Dragon are likely to clash frequently this year, Tiger.

Does that worry you? Not in the slightest. The typical Tiger finds such a battle of wills invigorating. Nothing the Tiger loves more than a huge adrenaline rush. Bring it on.

Yet when peace is restored and a truce hammered out, when the two of you commit to joining forces and working together, there's almost nothing you can't achieve. Your combined powers can move mountains. Together, you could change the world, and this year you get the chance.

Then there's the matter of the element of the year, which is Wood in 2024. Since the Dragon is also a Wood creature and the Tiger belongs to the Wood tribe as well, the two of you – despite your differences – have a lot in common deep down, and you're both in sync with the vibe of 2024.

All that Woodiness suits you, Tiger, particularly since the last two years have been awash with the Water element. So much so, it's become oppressive for many Tigers.

This is surprising because, at first glance, Water is a good thing for the Wood tribe since Water nourishes Wood and helps it grow. But water is also associated with, amongst other things, emotion. Consequently, over the last couple of years, many Tigers have found themselves plagued by emotional dramas.

Friends, relatives, colleagues, all have succumbed from time to time to behaviour Tiger regards as bizarre, bordering on hysterical.

Not only does the Tiger hate living in a soap opera, all that soggy dampness plays havoc with the Tiger's constitution. Many Tigers will have spent part of 2023 fighting niggling health issues, and the welcome 'drying out' of 2024 will come as a big relief.

So how does this play out down in the jungle of Tiger day-to-day life? Clashes and power struggles will arise at home and at work, Tiger, but of the fiery rather than the tearful type. Much easier for you to deal with.

There may be some complete breaks with the past as a result. Many a Tiger will part company with a job, two-faced friend, or relative or even a former residence.

Yet, this simply makes space for something better. The typical Tiger looks likely to join forces with a powerful ally. This may be someone you already know or someone you meet this year, but once the two of you combine your talents and start working together – full-time or as a side hustle – the sky's the limit. You could achieve something very significant. You could even become famous.

The bright lights and fancy titles don't interest most Tigers all that much, but accomplishing a worthwhile goal is a different matter. Get ready to give yourself a well-deserved pat on the back, Tiger.

Money and travel are likely to follow in the wake of this special mission as well as additional premises. Whether a new office, warehouse space, or just a simple garden shed, you're going to need a place to expand.

All in all, this is an eventful year, Tiger, one you'll remember for possibly decades to come.

What it Means to Be a Tiger

It's a wonderful thing to be a Tiger. Who could not be impressed with the great cat's magnificent striped coat, lithe yet powerful body, and arrogant, swaggering stride? We're all in awe of the Tiger – as well as being pretty scared, too.

In China, the sign is regarded as fortunate and noble. Fortunate because – let's face it – the Tiger owns the jungle and patrols his territory with savage grace; noble because it's believed the Tiger only kills when it's hungry or threatened. (Which may or may not be strictly true.)

Yet, the zodiac Tiger is also a contrary creature. You never know quite where you are with the typical Tiger. With a coat that's neither black nor orange – neither light nor dark – Tigers have two sides to their characters and can switch moods in an instant.

What's more, that striped pelt provides such perfect camouflage in the jungle; Tiger can melt into the shadows and become completely invisible, only to reappear without warning when least expected, to devastating effect.

Other signs instinctively know never to underestimate the Tiger.

Perhaps unsurprisingly, people born under this sign tend to attract good luck. They throw themselves into risky situations and escape unscathed, where others would come badly unstuck.

Tigers are fearless and restless. They like to be on the move and get bored easily. Wonderfully good-looking, Tigers tend to shine in company, and enjoy being surrounded by admirers, as they usually are. While perfectly happy in their own company and not craving attention, Tigers are confident and unfazed by a crowd. They take it as quite natural that other signs seek them out and want to hear their opinions.

The Tiger has a magnetic personality and can be highly entertaining, but they're also surprisingly moody – laughing and joking one minute, then flying into a rage over almost nothing the next. Despite this, the Tiger is very idealistic. Tiger can see what's wrong with the world and wants to put it right. What's more, courageous Tiger is quite prepared to get out there and put the necessary changes into action.

This is the sign of the daring revolutionary. The trouble is, Tigers can become so accustomed to getting away with audacious acts, they forget that – deep down – they're big cats and cats are said to have only nine lives. Push their luck too far, and sooner or later, Tiger can find it runs out.

Sporty and athletic, Tigers love to travel; when they're young, the typical Tiger is likely to want to be off to see the world. Even older Tigers insist on regular holidays and would happily take a sabbatical or 'adult gap year' if possible. Luxury travel or budget breaks, they don't really care as long as they're going somewhere different. They don't even mind going on their own, if necessary, as they're independent and self-assured; they are confident they'll find an interesting companion from time to time, along the way, if they need one.

Far too individual to be slaves to fashion, Tigers of both sexes still manage to look stylish and original in a pared-down, sleek sort of way. They can't be bothered with fiddly, fussy details, and they don't need to be because their natural features attract attention effortlessly. Similarly, the Tiger's home is attractive and unusual: full of intriguing objects and trophies that Tiger has collected during their adventures.

At work, if they manage to avoid quarrelling with the boss and walking out – a strong possibility as Tigers hate to be told what to do – Tigers tend to rise to the top of whatever field they happen to be in. But contradictory to the end, the Tiger is just as likely to reach the peak of their profession and then resign to try something new. In business, the Tiger can be creative, innovative, and utterly ruthless to competitors.

Best Jobs for Tiger in 2024

Charity Director

Activist

Lawyer

Social Worker

Investigative Journalist

Political Advisor

Perfect Partners

Cupid's arrow can strike anywhere at any time, of course, but once the novelty of new romance wears off, some relationships are easier to maintain than others. Here's a guide to the Tiger's compatibility with other signs.

Tiger with Tiger

The attraction between these two beautiful people is powerful. They understand each other so well, it's almost like looking in a mirror. They both like to walk on the wild side and will enjoy some exciting adventures together, but their moody interludes could lead to fierce quarrels. This match could be compulsive but stormy.

Tiger with Rabbit

Surprisingly, the Rabbit is not intimidated by Tiger's dangerous aura, and this attitude immediately appeals to Tiger who enjoys a challenge. Rabbit's calm presence and clever way with words keeps Tiger interested, while Rabbit finds Tiger's adventurous tales entertaining. With care, these two could get on well together for years.

Tiger with Dragon

The two biggest personalities in the zodiac would seem bound to clash. After all, these larger-than-life characters share so many similarities there's a danger they'd compete. Yet a relationship between the Tiger and Dragon often works very well. They understand each other's impulsive natures, but they're also different enough to supply the support the other needs. They'd make a formidable power couple.

Tiger with Snake

Not the best of romances. These two are so fundamentally different that any initial attraction is unlikely to last. Snake likes to bask and conserve energy while Tiger wants to leap right in and race about. Tiger takes in the big picture in a glance and is off to the next challenge while Snake likes to pause, delve beneath the surface, and consider. It wouldn't take long before these two annoy each other.

Tiger with Horse

This athletic pair get on pretty well. They both like physical pursuits, testing their strength out of doors or just enjoying the feel of the wind in their hair and the ground under their feet. True, Horse may not quite understand Tiger's plans for world domination, but it doesn't really matter. Horse is happy to be loyal to such a charismatic partner. As they're both moody, there could be rows, but making up is exciting.

Tiger with Goat

Tiger and Goat don't have a lot in common. While their aims and temperaments are quite different, they are both sociable creatures, and Goat wouldn't mind Tiger attracting all the attention when they're out together. Tiger, in return, would appreciate Goat's lack of jealousy and generosity of spirit. Yet, long-term, they're likely to drift apart as they follow their different interests.

Tiger with Monkey

Tiger can't help being intrigued by sparkling Monkey and Monkey is flattered by such interest. Who wouldn't enjoy being admired by such a fabulous creature? But irrepressible Monkey just can't help teasing and being teased is not a sensation Tiger is familiar with, nor appreciates. Unless the attraction is very strong, these two will wind each other up until they can bear it no longer and part.

Tiger with Rooster

The only feathered creature in the zodiac, the opulence and novelty of Rooster's appearance will draw Tiger like a magnet. What's more, deep down they are both quite serious-minded types so, on one level, they'll have much to share. Yet, despite this, they're not really on the same wavelength, and misunderstandings will keep recurring. Could be hard work.

Tiger with Dog

While not exactly opposites, these two are different enough to intrigue each other yet similar enough in basic outlook to get on well. Both Tiger and Dog are idealistic and uninterested in material gain yet where Dog can be nervous, Tiger's bold; and where Tiger attracts controversy, Dog will be loyal. This partnership could be lasting and valuable.

Tiger with Pig

Carefree Pig will love to bask in Tiger's impressive aura, while Tiger will feel good about protecting this charming but unworldly creature. They enjoy each other's company and Tiger, so focused on lofty matters will find Pig's compulsive shopping too trivial to worry about. This couple could do well together as long as Pig's fondness for cosy nights in doesn't make Tiger feel trapped.

Tiger with Rat

Sleek and clever Rat can easily attract Tiger's attention because the intelligent Tiger loves witty conversation. Yet these two are not natural partners. Tiger's not interested in Rat's latest bargain and has no wish to talk about it while Rat doesn't share Tiger's passion for changing the world. Still, if they can agree to step back and not get in each other's way, they could reach a good understanding.

Tiger with Ox

Not an easy match. Ox and Tiger could be on different planets. Fiery Tiger doesn't frighten Ox, and Tiger may admire Ox's strong, good looks and sincere nature, but they both need different things from life. Tiger wants to dash about creating big changes, while Ox reckons you get more done by buckling down where you happen to be and attending to the details. Clashes could abound.

Tiger Love 2024 Style

What can we say, Tiger? You've got it all. You're drop-dead gorgeous in a sleek, edgy way. You rock the most crazily outrageous mix of styles, yet somehow appear not wacky but years ahead of your time.

You're the one everyone wants to emulate, you're the one everyone wants to be with, you're the one everyone wants to be, full stop. And you know what? You don't even notice.

You're totally, completely your own person. You wouldn't change for anyone. That's what fascinates them so. No surprise, then, that both single and attached Tigers will attract their usual crowd of besotted admirers this year. Adoring fans are simply part of the big cat landscape.

And, as usual, the typical single Tiger is in no hurry to tie themselves down, though happy enough to allow a series of light romances. What's different this year is that in 2024, single Tigers consumed by the excitement of their grand scheme, find themselves thrown together with an attractive team-mate who shares their passion.

You may think you're too busy to socialise, but it looks like things will get pretty steamy at work.

Attached Tigers may find the Dragon/Tiger clash materialises at home in the form of repeated, high-volume discussions with their partner. As long as your partner is not the over-sensitive type, this is not necessarily a bad thing. All that tempestuous drama raises passions sky-high. The two of you could fall in love all over again.

Secrets of Success in 2024

This could be your big chance, Tiger. Admittedly, the year may start with more than the usual rows and power struggles. Colleagues and business contacts, for some reason, are acting difficult. Unreasonable demands are likely to be made. This is particularly awkward since irritation seethes very close to the surface of the Tiger pelt. You'll need to grit your teeth and keep silent many times – when you really want to let rip – if you're to avoid disaster.

Yet, if you keep a tight grip on that temper and think smart, huge potential awaits. Somewhere in the Tiger orbit lurks a talented, influential or idealistic person. This may be someone you already know, or it may be someone you meet in the coming months – but as well as possessing strength of character equal to your own, they also have skills that complement yours perfectly.

Separately, you're both likely to enjoy success, but together you can reach amazing heights. The two of you could achieve more than you ever dreamed possible.

You're not a natural for partnerships, Tiger. You don't suffer fools, and you like things done your way. You insist on it, in fact. Yet if you can find a way of compromising with this person, you'll be grateful for ever more when you see the results.

The Tiger Year at a Glance

January – Impatient Tiger. You're getting ready to pace. Progress has slowed, but it's just the post-festivity slump.

February – A clutch of Valentine cards coming your way? One's familiar, but one... you haven't a clue. A secret admirer?

March – A clash at work leads to an apology. You're on the right side.

April – Unusual events capture your interest. You sense a big chance. Think creatively.

May – Someone in your circle is being obstructive. They have their reasons, but do you agree? Bite your tongue while you find out more.

June – A brilliant idea strikes, and a romantic interlude beckons. What's not to like?

July – You're getting restless, but a work trip looks possible. You can make it happen. Lateral thinking works wonders.

August – You're in two minds about a new face in your orbit. Are they sincere or faking their charm? Give it time.

September – Overseas is calling your name. Get away if you possibly can. The more exotic, the better.

October – An unlikely partnership is working well. You never thought this could happen, but you're enjoying yourself.

November – Cash is raining down on the Tiger jungle. A pay rise or a win of some kind? Either way, you're not complaining.

December – Foreign festivities are appealing. Either Christmas abroad for many Tigers or an overseas face at the Christmas table.

Lucky colours for 2024: Emerald Green, Gold, Ruby

Lucky numbers for 2024: 6, 8

Three Takeaways

When provoked, count to ten.

Develop patience. Try mindfulness.

Make time for partying.

CHAPTER 13: THE RABBIT

Rabbit Years

2 February 1927 – 22 January 1928

19 February 1939 – 7 February 1940

6 February 1951 – 26 January 1952

25 January 1963 – 12 February 1964

11 February 1975 – 30 January 1976

29 January 1987 – 16 February 1988

6 February 1999 – 4 February 2000

3 February 2011 – 22 January 2012

22 January 2023 – 9 February 2024

8 February 2035 – 27 January 2036

26 January 2047 – 13 February 2048

Natural Element: Wood

Will 2024 be a Golden Year for the Rabbit?

Okay, Rabbit, this is the moment you've been waiting for. You can take off that crown, lock up 'The Ruler's' office door, kick out the remaining hangers-on, and skip off into the sunshine a free bunny.

If you're typical of your sign, 2023 was an interesting experience. You're probably glad you gave it a go, and you've done pretty well for yourself, but now you're even gladder to hand over the keys of the kingdom to the Dragon and escape for a well-earned break.

It's all very well being in charge, as the Rabbit was last year – you get to call the shots and insist on things being done your way – but after a while, the responsibility starts to wear you down. You also get the blame if things go wrong. Just look at what happened in 1963 when President Kennedy was assassinated; it's gone down forever in history as a Rabbit year. Most upsetting.

Yet, there's no point in taking these things personally, Rabbit. You've actually done very well in 2023 if you're typical of your sign. You've kept everything ticking over nicely in the bobtail realm; you've managed to guide things along at the pace you prefer. Many Rabbits will find cash mounting agreeably in their bank accounts as a result, while business Rabbits are counting healthy profits.

So, now, here we are in 2024, and you could be feeling a little nervous. The Dragon is another of those huge, overpowering creatures that could seem intimidating to a small, furry bunny. Yet, strangely, you're more likely to experience a wonderful sense of freedom.

For a start, the Dragon has no resentment towards the Rabbit. In fact, in the version of the Jade Emperor's race that describes Dragon helping Rabbit across the river (by blowing Rabbit's log to the bank), it's obvious the Dragon is very protective of the Rabbit. They may be too different to be great mates, but they have a lot of time for each other nonetheless.

So, this year, the Dragon's protective instincts will be on display as far as the Rabbit is concerned. The Dragon wants to help you, Rabbit, and shield you from harm.

In day-to-day life, this will probably play out as a sudden lifting of restrictions. Where many a Rabbit held back on various projects last year – in order to consolidate their position and build on what they'd achieved so far – now the barriers are down.

You are free to strike out in whatever fresh direction takes your fancy, Rabbit. Changing jobs was not advised last year unless absolutely necessary, but 2024 is different. Many Rabbits will apply for ambitious new roles and get them. Some will bask in surprising recognition at work – all the effort you put in in 2023 has been noticed at last! Others will either change careers altogether or diversify into several linked ventures.

Everything happens a bit faster than you're totally comfortable with, Rabbit, but you can cope.

At home, the people around you are urging changes in the Rabbit sphere. A bigger residence, more garden space, more family time, more holidays, a different car... They want your agreement, Rabbit. The

Bobtail friends are at it, too. They don't see enough of you; how about hanging out, going on a break, catching that new film in town?

It's good to be popular but, really! Yet if it all seems a tad overwhelming, Rabbit, you can blame it on the Wood element of the year added to the Dragon's forceful nature. The overriding impulse of the Wood element is to grow and expand, which also happens to be the Dragon's major goal. Put the two energies together – as they are this year – and the results are unstoppable.

No good digging your heels in, Rabbit. This year, you're being pushed to make major changes. As touched upon, a new home, new car, new workplace – all are up for grabs. And if you think your holidays will follow the same old format, think again. A totally different kind of break will come your way in 2024, Rabbit, and chances are you're going to love it.

Right now, all this may seem daunting, Rabbit, but never forget, you too belong to the Wood family just like your cosmic cousins – the Dragon and the Tiger. Unleash your inner big beast and see how you thrive.

What it Means to Be a Rabbit

We all love Rabbits, don't we? After the possibly dull Ox, and terrifying Tiger, the soft and pretty Rabbit seems like a welcome relief. We can all relate to the Rabbit. Big brown eyes, powder puff tail, cute little quivering nose, and an endearing way of hopping neatly around – nobody could take offence at the Rabbit.

In fact, nobody could feel threatened by the Rabbit in any way unless they happen to be a carrot, or a salad vegetable.

Yet, in the West, not all zodiac Rabbits are proud of their sign. They believe it suggests vulnerability and lack of drive. In the East, however, the Rabbit is appreciated for some very important qualities.

Like the Rat, Rabbits are brilliant survivors; they thrive and colonise in all manner of difficult terrains but, unlike the Rat, they manage to do this – mostly – without enraging or disgusting anyone, bar a few irritated farmers.

For all their cuddly looks, these are tough little creatures, frequently under-estimated. It's no accident that in the Chinese calendar, the defenceless, non-swimming Rabbit still manages to cross the river in fourth place, way ahead of stronger, abler creatures with seemingly much more going for them.

People born under this sign are never flashy or loud. Enter a crowded room, and the Rabbit wouldn't be the first person you notice. Yet, after a while, a stylish, immaculately-turned-out character would draw your eye. Classy and understated with perfect hair and graceful gestures – the typical Rabbit. This effortlessly polished aura is a gift. A Rabbit can emerge soaked to the skin from a rainstorm in a muddy field and within minutes appear clean, unruffled, and co-ordinated. Even Rabbits don't know how they do it. They're not even aware they *are* doing it.

Rabbits are refined with cultured tastes. They love beautiful things and art of all kinds, and hate to be surrounded by untidiness and disorder. Harmony is very important to the Rabbit – both visually and emotionally. People born in Rabbit years are sensitive in every way. They hate loud noises, loud voices, heavy traffic, and general ugliness. Quarrels can actually make them ill.

Yet this loathing of discord doesn't mean the Rabbit retires from the world. Rabbits somehow manage to end up near the centre of the action and tend to walk away with what they want, without appearing to have made any visible effort to get it.

Softly-spoken Rabbits are natural diplomats. Discreet and tactful, they can always find the right words; the perfect solutions to keep everybody happy. In fact, their powers of persuasion are so sophisticated that people usually do what Rabbit wants in the belief it's their own idea. This approach is so successful that Rabbit can't understand why other signs resort to argument and challenge, when so much more can be achieved through quiet conversation and compromise.

Rabbits tend to be brilliant strategists. When other egos get too distracted, jockeying for position and trying to be in charge for the task in hand, Rabbit deftly assesses the situation and has a plan worked out before the others have even agreed an agenda. Outwardly modest, Rabbits rarely admit to being ambitious, so they often end up being underestimated. Yet, privately, Rabbits can be single-minded and determined, even ruthless at times. These qualities, combined with their diplomatic skills and calm efficiency, seem to propel them smoothly to the top of whatever profession they've chosen.

Rabbits love their homes, which naturally are as beautiful and harmonious as they are. Home is a sanctuary and Rabbits take a lot of pleasure in choosing just the right pieces and décor to make their special place perfect, but in a comfortable way. Tidiness comes easily to them, and they can bring order to chaos quickly and neatly with the minimum of fuss. They enjoy entertaining – preferably small, informal gatherings of good friends – and they make wonderful hosts. Since they are such agreeable types, they're popular with everyone, and a Rabbit's invitation to dinner is accepted with eagerness.

When life is calm and secure, the Rabbit is perfectly happy to stay in one place. These types are not desperate for novelty though they do enjoy a relaxing holiday. Extreme sports are unlikely to appeal, but gentle exercise in beautiful surroundings soothes their nerves, and if they can take in an art gallery or a historic church followed by a delicious meal, they'd be truly contented bunnies.

Best Jobs for Rabbits 2024

Fashion designer

Nurse

Artist

Writer

Architect

Consultant

Perfect Partners

Cupid's arrow can strike anywhere at any time, of course, but once the novelty of new romance wears off, some relationships are easier to maintain than others. Here's a guide to the Rabbit's compatibility with other signs.

Rabbit with Rabbit

These two gorgeous creatures look like they're made for each other. Their relationship will always be calm, peaceful, and unruffled, and it goes without saying that their home could grace a glossy magazine. Yet though they never argue, the willingness of both partners to compromise could end up with neither ever quite doing what they want. Ultimately, they may find the spark goes out.

Rabbit with Dragon

Dragon is such a larger-than-life character, Rabbit could feel overwhelmed at times. Also, the Dragon can be rather noisy and over-dramatic, which would get on Rabbit's nerves. Yet they each admire the other's good points. If they could live next door to each other instead of under the same roof, a long-term relationship might work.

Rabbit with Snake

This subtle pair could make a good combination. They both understand the value of working behind the scenes and neither has any desire to wear themselves out on endless adventures. They share a love of art, fine things, and quiet pleasures, and they both enjoy an orderly home. These two could settle down very happily together.

Rabbit with Horse

This could be tricky. It's fairly unlikely that Horse and Rabbit would ever end up on a date, but if they did, and there was a strong attraction, it could lead to a love/hate relationship. Rabbit's neat and tidy ways would enrage Horse, and Horse's unpredictable moods and over-the-top reactions would annoy Rabbit. Soon, Horse is likely to bolt for the hills or Rabbit retreat to its burrow.

Rabbit with Goat

Happy-go-lucky Goat is very appealing to Rabbit, particularly as deep-down Rabbit is a bit of a worrier. They're both sociable without needing to be the centre of attention and would be happy to people-watch for hours and then cheerfully compare notes afterwards. Goat is tolerant of Rabbit's need for some regular alone time to recharge too, so this couple could be a successful match.

Rabbit with Monkey

Mercurial Monkey doesn't really 'get' Rabbit. The Monkey can appreciate how well Rabbit operates and sees this approach gets good results, but it's all too picky and slow for Monkey. Rabbit, on the other hand, is amused by Monkey's quick wit and clever ways but deplores Monkey's slapdash, sometimes devious tactics. Very unlikely to work out.

Rabbit with Rooster

Another difficult match. However unfair it seems, Rooster comes over as loud, boastful, and uncouth to Rabbit, while Rabbit appears dull, staid, and insufficiently admiring of Rooster's fine feathers to appeal to Rooster. These two just can't see below the surface of the other, and it would be surprising if they ended up together. Only to be considered by the very determined.

Rabbit with Dog

Despite the fact that in the outside world Rabbit could easily end up as Dog's dinner, the astrological pair get on surprisingly well. Dog appreciates Rabbit's careful, efficient ways and soft voice, while Rabbit admires Dog's energy and good intentions. Dog's lack of interest in the finer points of interior design might try Rabbit's patience, but with a little work these two could reach an understanding.

Rabbit with Pig

Pig is not quite as interested in fine dining as Rabbit being as happy to scoff a burger as a Cordon Bleu creation, but their shared love of the good things in life makes these two happy companions. Once again, Pig's spending habits might irritate Rabbit, but not too much as Rabbit is quite willing to splurge on lovely things for the home. A relationship would work well.

Rabbit with Rat

Rat finds Rabbit intriguing. Here is an attractive, stylish creature that doesn't feel the need to be pushy or take centre stage yet somehow manages to be at the heart of things, while Rabbit is flattered and entertained by witty Rat's attention. These two respect each other but long-term, Rat could be too overpowering unless they both agree to give each other space.

Rabbit with Ox

Ox finds Rabbit rather cute and appealing. Whether male or female, there's something about Rabbit's inner fluffiness that brings out Ox's highly-developed protective instincts. Rabbit, meanwhile, loves the Ox's reassuring presence, and the sense of security Ox provides. These two could get on very well together as long as refined Rabbit can overlook Ox's occasional down-to-earth – Rabbit might say 'coarse' – observations.

Rabbit with Tiger

Surprisingly, the Rabbit is not intimidated by Tiger's dangerous aura and this attitude immediately appeals to Tiger who enjoys a challenge. Rabbit's calm presence and clever way with words keeps Tiger interested, while Rabbit finds Tiger's adventurous tales entertaining. With care, these two could get on well together for years.

Rabbit Love 2024 Style

The delicious Rabbit is a sight to behold. Simple elegance, innately stylish, with an exquisite way of blending one colour with another. There are no harsh lines or jarring details. The typical Rabbit, dressed for an occasion, takes the breath away.

The only trouble is, other signs are so busy admiring your perfect looks, Rabbit, that they hesitate to get too close. This isn't really too much of a problem for the clever Rabbit, though. You have a mysterious way of installing yourself quietly beside an object of your interest and somehow ending up leaving as their partner.

This year, single Rabbits may develop a hankering to settle down and create a new household. There will be no shortage of opportunities, but (of course) the discriminating Rabbit is looking for someone very special. You may well find them in 2024, Rabbit. Accept all invitations involving outdoor celebrations.

Attached Rabbits could find themselves slightly stressed with their partner's determination to rearrange the Rabbit residence or relocate altogether. Oh, and possibly increase the Rabbit household, as well. You might as well go with the flow, Rabbit. It's going to happen anyway, so keep the peace.

Secrets of Success in 2024

Better set the alarm clock a little earlier, Rabbit, and maybe schedule in some meditation breaks as well. The Dragon is about to waft you to success this year, as long as you play by Dragon rules.

The Dragon believes in working hard and playing hard – which can be exhausting for a sensitive Rabbit – which is where the meditation breaks come in.

Basically, the Dragon demands a bold approach, a certain calculated risk-taking and a willingness to change. Not that the Rabbit disagrees with any of these things; it's just that your interpretation of them is usually a much paler, toned-down version of what Dragon has in mind.

So, this year, think BIG, Rabbit. Whatever you've got in mind, double it, do it faster, do it further, and carry it on for longer than you originally envisioned. And if you can rope in some other signs to help you, so much the better.

Resist the temptation to relax from your efforts with a little light gambling, too, Rabbit. While the Dragon encourages investing in your business, throwing your money away is a big no-no.

But, stick to the Dragon rules, and that famous Dragon luck will pave your path with gold into 2025.

The Rabbit Year at a Glance

January – An older person takes you under their wing. You can benefit from their wisdom and guidance.

February – A change of job is in the air. Is this the right role for you, or should you bide your time? Follow your instincts.

March – Responsibilities mount, but so do your rewards. Keep calm. You can cope.

April – A fresh face on the scene is energising your circle. You can't help being swept along. Looks like fun.

May – The possibility of a new job offer comes your way, along with a new romance. Exciting times.

June – A changeable person is wearing you down. You just can't please them. Best to make your own decision and stick to it.

July – Time for a trip. A partner books a surprise break. It's not what you'd usually choose, but you surprise yourself.

August – A possible business venture is proposed. It's a bit wild, but don't dismiss it instantly. There could be hidden potential.

September – Romance could get complicated. You seem to be entangled with more than one love. Diplomatic skills required.

October – Unexpected opportunities arrive. Career prospects are rocketing. Yes, it is really happening, Rabbit. Enjoy.

November – You or your partner are becoming foodies. MasterChef at home or a food festival to sample. Tuck in!

December – Big festivities in the Rabbit residence. You've got a lot to celebrate. Champagne, all round!

Lucky colours for 2024: Aqua, Pink, Green

Lucky numbers for 2024: 4, 10, 8

Three Takeaways

Create a cosy Rabbit den.

Prioritise family get-togethers.

Get daring at work.

CHAPTER 14: BUT THEN THERE'S SO MUCH MORE TO YOU

So now you know your animal sign, but possibly you're thinking – okay, but how can everyone born in the same year as me have the same personality as me?

You've only got to think back to your class at school, full of children the same age as you, to know this can't be true. And you're absolutely right. What's more, Chinese astrologers agree with you. For this reason, in Chinese astrology, your birth year is only the beginning. The month you were born and the hour of your birth are also ruled by the twelve zodiac animals – and not necessarily the same animal that rules your birth year.

These other animals then go on to modify the qualities of your basic year personality. So, someone born in an extrovert Tiger year but at the time of day ruled by the quieter Ox, and in the month of the softly spoken Snake, for instance, would very likely find their risk-taking Tiger qualities much toned down and enhanced by a few other calmer, more subtle traits.

By combining these three important influences, you get a much more accurate and detailed picture of the complex and unique person you really are. These calculations lead to so many permutations it soon becomes clear how people born in the same year can share various similarities, yet still remain quite different from each other.

What's more, the other animals linked to your date of birth can also have a bearing on how successful you will be in any year and how well you get on with people from other signs. Traditionally, the Horse and the Rabbit don't get on well together, for instance, so you'd expect two people born in these years to be unlikely to end up good friends. Yet if both individuals had other compatible signs in their charts, they could find themselves surprisingly warming to each other.

This is how it works:

Your Outer Animal – (Birth Year | Creates Your First Impression)

You're probably completely unaware of it, but when people meet you for the first time, they will sense the qualities represented by the animal that ruled your birth year. Your Outer Animal and its personality influence the way you appear to the outside world. Your Outer animal is your public face. You may not feel the least bit like this creature deep down, and you may wonder why nobody seems to understand the real you. Why is it that people always seem to underestimate you, or perhaps overestimate you, you may ask yourself frequently. The reason is that you just can't help giving the impression of your birth-year animal and people will tend to see you and think of you in this way – especially if they themselves were born in other years.

Your Inner Animal – (Birth Month I The Private You)

Your Inner Animal is the animal that rules the month in which you were born. The personality of this creature tells you a lot about how you feel inside, what motivates you, and how you tend to live your life. When you're out in the world and want to present yourself in the best light, it's easy for you to project the finest talents of your birth-year animal. You've got them at your fingertips. But at home, with no one you need to impress, your Inner Animal comes to the fore. You can kick back and relax. You may find you have abilities and interests that no one at work would ever guess. Only your closest friends and loved ones are likely to get to know your Inner Animal.

By now you know your Outer Animal so you can move on to find your Inner Animal from the chart below:

Month of Birth - Your Inner Animal

January – the Ox

February – the Tiger

March – the Rabbit

April – the Dragon

May – the Snake

June – the Horse

July – the Goat

August – the Monkey

September – the Rooster

October – the Dog

November – the Pig

December – the Rat

Your Secret Animal – (Birth Hour | The Still, Small Voice Within)

Your secret animal rules the time you were born. Each 24-hour period is divided into 12, two-hour time-slots and each slot is believed to be ruled by a particular animal. This animal represents the deepest, most secret part of you. It's possibly the most intimate, individual part of you as it marks the moment you first entered the world and became 'you'. This animal is possibly your conscience and your inspiration. It might represent qualities you'd like to have or sometimes fail to live up to. Chances are, no one else will ever meet your Secret Animal.

For your Secret Animal check out the time of your birth:

Hours of Birth – Your Secret Animal

1 am – 3 am – the Ox

3 am – 5 am – the Tiger

5 am – 7 am – the Rabbit

7 am – 9 am – the Dragon

9 am – 11 am – the Snake

11 am – 1.00 pm – the Horse

1.00 pm – 3.00 pm – the Goat

3.00 pm – 5.00 pm – the Monkey

5.00 pm – 7.00 pm – the Rooster

7.00 pm – 9.00 pm – the Dog

9.00 pm – 11.00 pm – the Pig

11.00 pm – 1.00 am – the Rat

When you've found your other animals, go back to the previous chapters and read the sections on those particular signs. You may well discover talents and traits that you recognise immediately as belonging to you in addition to those mentioned in your birth year. It could also be that your Inner Animal or your Secret Animal is the same as your Year animal. A Dragon born at 8 am in the morning, for instance, will be a secret Dragon inside as well as outside, because the hours between 7 am and 9 am are ruled by the Dragon.

When this happens, it suggests that the positive and the less positive attributes of the Dragon will be held in harmony, so this particular Dragon ends up being very well balanced.

You might also like to look at your new animal's compatibility with other signs and see where you might be able to widen your circle of friends and improve your love life.

CHAPTER 15: IN YOUR ELEMENT

There's no doubt about it: Chinese astrology has many layers. But then we all recognise that we have many facets to our personalities, too. We are all more complicated than we might first appear. And more unique, as well.

It turns out that even people who share the same Chinese zodiac sign are not identical to people with the same sign but born in different years. A Dragon born in 1964, for instance, will express their Dragon personality in a slightly different way to a Dragon born in 1976. This is not simply down to the influence of the other animals in their chart, it's because each year is also believed to be ruled by one of the five Chinese 'elements', as well as the year animal.

These elements are known as Water, Wood, Fire, Earth, and Metal.

Each element is thought to contain special qualities which are bestowed onto people born in the year it ruled, in addition to the qualities of their animal sign.

Since there are 12 signs endlessly rotating, and five elements, the same animal and element pairing only recurs once every 60 years. Which is why babies born in this 2024 Year of the Green Dragon are unlikely to grow up remembering much about other Green Dragons from the previous generation. Those senior Green Dragons will already be 60 years old when the baby Green Dragons are born.

In years gone by, when life expectancy was lower, chances are there would only ever be one generation of a particular combined sign and element alive in the world at a time.

Find Your Element from the Chart Below:

The 1920s

5 February 1924 – 24 January 1925 | RAT | WOOD

25 January 1925 – 12 February 1926 | OX | WOOD

13 February 1926 – 1 February 1927 | TIGER | FIRE

2 February 1927 – 22 January 1928 | RABBIT | FIRE

23 January 1928 – 9 February 1929 | DRAGON | EARTH

10 February 1929 – 29 January 1930 | SNAKE | EARTH

The 1930s

30 January 1930 – 16 February 1931 | HORSE | METAL

17 February 1931 – 5 February 1932 | GOAT | METAL

6 February 1932 – 25 January 1933 | MONKEY | WATER

26 January 1933 – 13 February 1934 | ROOSTER | WATER

14 February 1934 – 3 February 1935 | DOG | WOOD

4 February 1935 – 23 January 1936 | PIG | WOOD

24 January 1936 – 10 February 1937 | RAT | FIRE

11 February 1937 – 30 January 1938 | OX | FIRE

31 January 1938 – 18 February 1939 | TIGER | EARTH

19 February 1939 – 7 February 1940 | RABBIT | EARTH

The 1940s

8 February 1940 – 26 January 1941 | DRAGON | METAL

27 January 1941 – 14 February 1942 | SNAKE | METAL

15 February 1942 – 4 February 1943 | HORSE | WATER

5 February 1943 – 24 January 1944 | GOAT | WATER

25 January 1944 – 12 February 1945 | MONKEY | WOOD

13 February 1945 – 1 February 1946 | ROOSTER | WOOD

2 February 1946 – 21 January 1947 | DOG | FIRE

22 January 1947 – 9 February 1948 | PIG | FIRE

10 February 1948 – 28 January 1949 | RAT | EARTH

29 January 1949 – 16 February 1950 | OX | EARTH

The 1950s

17 February 1950 – 5 February 1951 | TIGER | METAL

6 February 1951 – 26 January 1952 | RABBIT | METAL

27 January 1952 – 13 February 1953 | DRAGON | WATER

14 February 1953 – 2 February 1954 | SNAKE | WATER

3 February 1954 – 23 January 1955 | HORSE | WOOD

24 January 1955 – 11 February 1956 | GOAT | WOOD

12 February 1956 – 30 January 1957 | MONKEY | FIRE

31 January 1957 – 17 February 1958 | ROOSTER | FIRE

18 February 1958 – 7 February 1959 | DOG | EARTH

8 February 1959 – 27 January 1960 | PIG | EARTH

The 1960s

28 January 1960 – 14 February 1961 | RAT | METAL

15 February 1961 – 4 February 1962 | OX | METAL

5 February 1962 – 24 January 1963 | TIGER | WATER

25 January 1963 – 12 February 1964 | RABBIT | WATER

13 February 1964 – 1 February 1965 | DRAGON | WOOD

2 February 1965 – 20 January 1966 | SNAKE | WOOD

21 January 1966 – 8 February 1967 | HORSE | FIRE

9 February 1967 – 29 January 1968 | GOAT | FIRE

30 January 1968 – 16 February 1969 | MONKEY | EARTH

17 February 1969 – 5 February 1970 | ROOSTER | EARTH

The 1970s

6 February 1970 – 26 January 1971 | DOG | METAL

27 January 1971 – 14 February 1972 | PIG | METAL

15 February 1972 – 2 February 1973 | RAT | WATER

3 February 1973 – 22 January 1974 | OX | WATER

23 January 1974 – 10 February 1975 | TIGER | WOOD

11 February 1975 – 30 January 1976 | RABBIT | WOOD

31 January 1976 – 17 February 1977 | DRAGON | FIRE

18 February 1977 – 6 February 1978 | SNAKE | FIRE

7 February 1978 – 27 January 1979 | HORSE | EARTH

28 January 1979 – 15 February 1980 | GOAT | EARTH

The 1980s

16 February 1980 – 4 February 1981 | MONKEY | METAL

5 February 1981 – 24 January 1982 | ROOSTER | METAL

25 January 1982 – 12 February 1983 | DOG | WATER

13 February 1983 – 1 February 1984 | PIG | WATER

2 February 1984 – 19 February 1985 | RAT | WOOD

20 February 1985 – 8 February 1986 | OX | WOOD

9 February 1986 – 28 January 1987 | TIGER | FIRE

29 January 1987 – 16 February 1988 | RABBIT | FIRE

17 February 1988 – 5 February 1989 | DRAGON | EARTH

6 February 1989 – 26 January 1990 | SNAKE | EARTH

The 1990s

27 January 1990 – 14 February 1991 | HORSE | METAL

15 February 1991 – 3 February 1992 | GOAT | METAL

4 February 1992 – 22 January 1993 | MONKEY | WATER

23 January 1993 – 9 February 1994 | ROOSTER | WATER

10 February 1994 – 30 January 1995 | DOG | WOOD

31 January 1995 – 18 February 1996 | PIG | WOOD

19 February 1996 – 7 February 1997 | RAT | FIRE

8 February 1997 – 27 January 1998 | OX | FIRE

28 January 1998 – 5 February 1999 | TIGER | EARTH

6 February 1999 – 4 February 2000 | RABBIT | EARTH

The 2000s

5 February 2000 – 23 January 2001 | DRAGON | METAL

24 January 2001 – 11 February 2002 | SNAKE | METAL

12 February 2002 – 31 January 2003 | HORSE | WATER

1 February 2003 – 21 January 2004 | GOAT | WATER

22 January 2004 – 8 February 2005 | MONKEY | WOOD

9 February 2005 – 28 January 2006 | ROOSTER | WOOD

29 January 2006 – 17 February 2007 | DOG | FIRE

18 February 2007 – 6 February 2008 | PIG | FIRE

7 February 2008 – 25 January 2009 | RAT | EARTH

26 January 2009 – 13 February 2010 | OX | EARTH

The 2010s

14 February 2010 – 2 February 2011 | TIGER | METAL

3 February 2011 – 22 January 2012 | RABBIT | METAL

23 January 2012 – 9 February 2013 | DRAGON | WATER

10 February 2013 – 30 January 2014 | SNAKE | WATER

31 January 2014 – 18 February 2015 | HORSE | WOOD

19 February 2015 – 7 February 2016 | GOAT | WOOD

8 February 2016 – 27 January 2017 | MONKEY | FIRE

28 January 2017 – 15 February 2018 | ROOSTER | FIRE

16 February 2018 – 4 February 2019 | DOG | EARTH

5 February 2019 – 24 January 2020 | PIG | EARTH

The 2020s

25 January 2020 – 11 February 2021 | RAT | METAL

12 February 2021 – 1 February 2022 | OX | METAL

2 February 2022 – 21 January 2023 | TIGER | WATER

22 January 2023 – 9 February 2024 | RABBIT | WATER

10 February 2024 – 28 January 2025 | DRAGON | WOOD

29 January 2025 – 16 February 2026 | SNAKE | WOOD

17 February 2026 – 5 February 2027 | HORSE | FIRE

6 February 2027 – 25 January 2028 | GOAT | FIRE

26 January 2028 – 12 February 2029 | MONKEY | EARTH

13 February 2029 – 2 February 2030 | ROOSTER | EARTH

You may have noticed that the 'natural' basic element of your sign is not necessarily the same as the element of the year you were born. Don't worry about this. The element of your birth year takes precedence, though you could also read the qualities assigned to the natural element as well, as these will be relevant to your personality but to a lesser degree.

Metal

Metal is the element associated in China with gold and wealth. So, if you are a Metal child, you will be very good at accumulating money. The Metal individual is ambitious, even if their animal sign is not particularly career-minded. The Metal-born version of an unworldly sign will still somehow have an eye for a bargain or a good investment; they'll manage to buy at the right time when prices are low and be moved to sell just as the price is peaking. If they want to get rid of unwanted items, they'll potter along to a car boot sale and without appearing to try, somehow make a killing, selling the lot while stalls around them struggle for attention. Career-minded signs with the element Metal have to be careful they don't overdo things. They have a tendency to become workaholics. Wealth will certainly flow, but it could be at the expense of family harmony and social life.

The element of Metal adds power, drive, and tenacity to whatever sign it influences so if you were born in a Metal year, you'll never lack cash for long.

Water

Water is the element associated with communication, creativity, and the emotions. Water has a knack of flowing around obstacles, finding routes that are not obvious to the naked eye and seeping into the smallest cracks. So if you're a Water child, you'll be very good at getting what you want in an oblique, unchallenging way. You are one of nature's lateral thinkers. You are also wonderful with people. You're sympathetic, empathetic, and can always find the right words at the right time. You can also be highly persuasive, but in such a subtle way nobody notices your influence or input. They think the whole thing was their own idea.

People born in Water years are very creative and extremely intuitive. They don't know where their inspiration comes from, but somehow ideas just pour into their brains. Many artists were born in Water years.

Animal signs that are normally regarded as a little impatient and tactless have their rough edges smoothed when they appear in a Water year. People born in these years will be more diplomatic, artistic, and amiable than other versions of their fellow signs. And if you were born in a naturally sensitive, emotional sign, in a Water year, you'll be so intuitive you're probably psychic. Yet just as water can fall as gentle nurturing rain, or a raging destructive flood, so Water types need to take care not to let their emotions run away with them or to allow themselves to use their persuasive skills to be too manipulative.

Wood

Wood is the element associated with growth and expansion. In Chinese astrology, Wood doesn't primarily refer to the inert variety used to make floorboards and furniture, it represents living, flourishing trees and smaller plants, all pushing out of the earth and growing towards the sky.

Wood is represented by the colour green, not brown. If you're a Wood child, you're likely to be honest, generous, and friendly. You think BIG and like to be involved in numerous projects, often at the same time.

Wood people are practical yet imaginative and able to enlist the support of others simply by the sincerity and enthusiasm with which they tackle their plans. Yet even though they're always busy with a project, they somehow radiate calm, stability, and confidence. There's a sense of the timeless serenity of a big old tree about Wood people. Other signs instinctively trust them and look to them for guidance.

Animal signs that could be prone to nervousness or impulsive behaviour tend to be calmer and more productive in Wood year versions, while signs whose natural element is also Wood could well end up leaders of vast teams or business empires. Wood people tend to sail smoothly through life, but they must guard against becoming either stubborn or unyielding as they grow older or alternatively, saying 'yes' to every new plan and overextending themselves.

Fire

Fire is the element associated with dynamism, strength, and persistence. Fire demands action, movement, and expansion. It also creates a huge amount of heat. Fire is precious when it warms our homes and cooks our food, and it possesses a savage beauty that's endlessly fascinating. Yet it's also highly dangerous and destructive if it gets out of control. Something of this ambivalent quality is evident in Fire children.

People born in Fire years tend to be immensely attractive, magnetic types. Other signs are drawn to them. Yet there is always a hint of danger, of unpredictability, about them. You never know quite where you are with a Fire year sign and in a way, this is part of their fascination.

People born in Fire years like to get things done. They are extroverted and bold and impatient for action. They are brilliant at getting things started and energising people and projects. Quieter signs born in a Fire year are more dynamic, outspoken, and energetic than their fellow sign cousins, while extrovert signs positively blaze with exuberance and confidence when Fire is added to the mix.

People born in Fire years will always be noticed, but they should try to remember they tend to be impatient and impulsive. Develop a habit of pausing to take a deep breath to consider things, before rushing in, and you won't get burned.

Earth

Earth is the element associated with patience, stability, and practicality. This may not sound exciting but, in Chinese astrology, Earth is at the centre of everything: the heart of the planet. Earth year children are strong, hardworking personalities. They will persist with a task if it's worthwhile and never give up until it's complete. They create structure and balance, and they have very nurturing instincts.

Women born in Earth years make wonderful mothers, and if they're not mothering actual children, they'll be mothering their colleagues at work, or their friends and relatives, while also filling their homes with houseplants and raising vegetables in the garden if at all possible.

Other signs like being around Earth types as they exude a sense of security. Earth people don't like change, and they strive to keep their lives settled and harmonious. They are deeply kind and caring and immensely honest. Tact is not one of their strong points, however. They will always say what they think, so if you don't want the unvarnished truth, better not to ask!

Earth lends patience and stability to the more flighty, over-emotional signs, and rock-solid integrity to the others. Earth people will be sought-after in whatever field they choose to enter, but they must take care not to become too stubborn. Make a point of seeking out and listening to a wide range of varying opinions before setting a decision in stone.

Yin and Yang

As you looked down the table of years and elements, you may have noticed that the elements came in pairs. Each element was repeated the following year. If the Monkey was Water one year, it would be followed immediately the next year by the Rooster, also Water.

This is because of Yin and Yang – the mysterious but vital forces that, in Chinese philosophy, are believed to control the planet and probably the whole universe. They can be thought of as positive and negative, light and dark, masculine and feminine, night and day, etc. but the important point is that everything is either Yin or Yang; the two forces complement each other and both are equally important because only together do they make up the whole. For peace and harmony to be achieved, both forces need to be in balance.

Each of the animal signs is believed to be either Yin or Yang and because of the need for balance and harmony, they alternate through the years. Six of the 12 signs are Yin and six are Yang and since Yang represents extrovert, dominant energy, the Yang sign is first, followed by the Yin sign which represents quiet, passive force. A Yang sign is always followed by a Yin sign throughout the cycle.

The Yang signs are:

Rat

Tiger

Dragon

Horse

Monkey

Dog

The Yin Signs are

Ox

Rabbit

Snake

Goat

Rooster

Pig

Although Yang is seen as a masculine energy, and Yin a feminine energy, in reality, whether you are male or female, everyone has a mixture of Yin and Yang within them. If you need to know, quickly, whether your sign is Yin or Yang just check your birth year. If it ends in an even number (or 0) your sign is Yang. If it ends in an odd number, your sign is Yin. (The only exception is if you're born in late January or early February and according to Chinese astrology you belong to the year before).

In general, Yang signs tend to be extrovert, action-oriented types while Yin signs are gentler, more thoughtful, and patient.

So, as balance is essential when an element controls a period of time, it needs to express itself in its stronger Yang form in a Yang year as well as in its gentler Yin form in a Yin year, to be complete.

This year of the Black Water Rabbit completes the round of the Water element. Last year it was in its Yang form accompanied by the Tiger, now it draws to a close in its Yin form with the Water Rabbit.

Next year the Wood element will begin and Water will not come round again until 2032.

But why do elements have two forms? It's to take into account the great variations in strength encompassed by an element. The difference between a candle flame and a raging inferno – both belonging to Fire; or a great oak tree and a blade of grass – both belonging to the Wood element. Each has to get the chance to be expressed to create balance.

So, in Yang years, the influence of the ruling element will be particularly strong. In Yin years, the same element expresses itself in its gentler form.

Friendly Elements

Just as some signs get on well together and others don't, so some elements work well together while others don't. These are the elements that exist in harmony:

METAL likes EARTH and WATER

WATER likes METAL and WOOD

WOOD likes WATER and FIRE

FIRE likes WOOD and EARTH

EARTH likes FIRE and METAL

The reason for these friendly partnerships is believed to be the natural, productive cycle. Water nourishes Wood and makes plants grow, Wood provides fuel for Fire, Fire produces ash which is a type of Earth, Earth can be melted or mined to produce Metal while Metal contains or carries Water in a bucket.

So, Water supports Wood, Wood supports Fire, Fire supports Earth, Earth supports Metal and Metal supports Water.

Unfriendly Elements

But since everything has to be in balance, all the friendly elements are opposed by the same number of unfriendly elements. These are the elements that are not in harmony:

METAL dislikes WOOD and FIRE

WATER dislikes FIRE and EARTH

WOOD dislikes EARTH and METAL

FIRE dislikes METAL and WATER

EARTH dislikes WOOD and WATER

The reason some elements don't get on is down to the destructive cycle which is: Water puts out Fire and is absorbed by Earth, Wood breaks up Earth (with its strong roots) and is harmed by Metal tools, Metal is melted by Fire and can cut down Wood.

So, if someone just seems to rub you up the wrong way, for no logical reason, it could be that your elements clash.

CHAPTER 16: WESTERN HOROSCOPES AND CHINESE HOROSCOPES – THE LINK

So now, hopefully, you'll have all the tools you need to create your very own, personal, multi-faceted Chinese horoscope. But does that mean the Western-style astrological sign that you're more familiar with is no longer relevant?

Not necessarily. Purists may not agree, but the odd thing is there does seem to be an overlap between a person's Western birth sign and their Chinese birth month sign; the two together can add yet another interesting layer to the basic birth year personality.

A Rabbit born under the Western sign of Leo may turn out to be very different on the surface, to a Rabbit born under the Western sign of Pisces for instance.

Of course, Chinese astrology already takes this into account by including the season of birth in a full chart, but we can possibly refine the system even further by adding the characteristics we've learned from our Western Sun Signs into the jigsaw.

If you'd like to put this theory to the test, simply find your Chinese year sign and then look up your Western Astrological sign within it, from the list below. While you're at it, why not check out the readings for your partner and friends too? You could be amazed at how accurate the results turn out to be.

Dragon

Aries Dragon

The Dragon is already a powerful sign, but when the lively influence of Aries is added, you have a positively devastating individual. These are the types that others either love or loathe. Strong, confident people can cope happily with the Aries Dragon, but more timid souls are terrified. The Aries Dragon himself is quite unaware of the reaction he causes. He goes busily on his way oblivious of the earthquakes all around him. These types have to guard against arrogance, particularly since they have quite a lot to be arrogant about. They also have a tendency to get bored easily and move on to new projects without completing the old, which is a pity since they can accomplish much if they persevere.

Taurus Dragon

There is something magnificent about the Taurus Dragon. Large, expansive types, they move easily around the social scene spreading bonhomie wherever they go. Not the most sensitive of individuals, they find it difficult to assess the moods of others and assume everyone else feels the same way they do. Should it be brought to their attention that someone is unhappy, however, they will move heaven and earth to cheer them up. These types are reliable and conscientious and always keep their promises.

Gemini Dragon

Dragons may not have the quickest minds in the Chinese zodiac, but Gemini Dragons are speedier than most. They are jovial types with a brilliant sense of humour. In fact, they can cleverly joke others into doing what they want. These types have no need for physical force to get their own way; they use laughter instead. At times, Gemini Dragons can be almost devious, which is unusual for a Dragon but nobody really minds their schemes. They give everyone such a good time on the way it's worth doing what they want for the sheer entertainment.

Cancer Dragon

Cautious Cancer and flamboyant Dragon make a surprisingly good combination. Cancer holds Dragon back where he might go too far, while Dragon endows the Crab with exuberance and style. These types like to help others make the most of themselves, but they are also high achievers in their own right. Without upsetting anyone, Cancer Dragons tend to zoom to the top faster than most.

Leo Dragon

This Dragon is so dazzling you need sunglasses to look at him. The proud, glorious Lion combined with the magnificent Dragon is an extraordinary combination, and it's fortunate it only comes around once every twelve years. Too many of such splendid creatures would be hard to take. Leo Dragons really do have star quality, and they know it. They demand to be the centre of attention and praise is like oxygen to them – they can't live without it. Yet they have generous hearts, and if anyone is in trouble, Leo Dragon will be the first to rush to their assistance.

Virgo Dragon

Unusually for a Dragon, the Virgo variety can get quite aggressive if crossed, but this doesn't often happen as very few people would dare take on such a daunting beast. These types are immensely clever in business. They steadily add acquisition to shrewd acquisition until they end up seriously rich. They are wilier than most Dragons who have a surprisingly naive streak, and they make the most of it. These types just can't help becoming successful in whatever they undertake.

Libra Dragon

Dragons are not usually too bothered about trifles such as fine clothes and wallpaper. In fact, some older, more absent-minded Dragons have been known to go shopping in their slippers having forgotten to take them off. The exception is the Dragon born under the sign of Libra. These types are more down to earth and see the sense in putting on a good show for others. They take the trouble to choose smart clothes and keep them looking that way at all times. They are also more intuitive and are not easily fooled by others.

Scorpio Dragon

Handling money is not a Dragon strong point, but the Scorpio variety has more ability in this direction than most. Scorpio Dragons enjoy amassing cash. Rather like their legendary namesakes who hoard treasure in their lairs, Scorpio Dragons like to build substantial nest-eggs and keep them close at hand where they can admire them regularly.

These types can also be a little stingy financially, not out of true meanness but simply because they don't like to see their carefully guarded heap diminish in size. Once they understand the importance of a purchase, however, they can be just as generous as their brothers and sisters.

Sagittarius Dragon

When Sagittarius joins the Dragon, the combination produces a real livewire, a true daredevil. The antics of the Sagittarius Dragon, when young, will give their mothers nightmares and later drive their partners to drink. These types can't resist a challenge, particularly a dangerous one. They will climb mountain peaks, leap off cliffs on a hang-glider and try a spot of bungee-jumping to enliven a dull moment. It's no good expecting these types to sit down with a good book; they just can't keep still. However, surrounded by friends, dashing from one perilous venture to the next, the Sagittarius Dragon is one of the happiest people around.

Capricorn Dragon

The Capricorn Dragon looks back at his Sagittarian brother in horror. He simply can't understand the need for such pranks. Being Dragons, these types are bold, but the influence of Capricorn ensures that they are never foolhardy. They look before they leap and occasionally miss a good deal because they stop to check the fine print. They are not the most intuitive of creatures, but show them a needy soul and they will efficiently do whatever's necessary to help. The Capricorn Dragon is a highly effective creature.

Aquarius Dragon

Happy go lucky types, the Aquarius Dragons are usually surrounded by people. Honest and hardworking, they will put in just as much effort for very little cash as they will for a great deal. If someone asks them to do a job and they agree to do it, they will move heaven and earth to fulfil their obligations even if it is not in their best interests to do so. However, they're not suited to routine, and if a task doesn't interest them, they will avoid it at all costs no matter how well paid it might be. Not particularly interested in money for its own sake, these types are sociable and easy to get along with. They are often highly talented in some way.

Pisces Dragon

Pisces Dragons, on the other hand, are surprisingly good with cash. Despite their often vague, good-humoured exteriors these types have excellent financial brains and seem to know just what to do to increase their savings. They are first in the queue when bargains are to be found, and they seem to sense what the next money-making trend is going to be before anyone else has thought of it. These types often end up quite wealthy and excel, particularly, in artistic fields.

Snake

Aries Snake

Generally speaking, Snakes tend to lack energy, so the influence of dynamic Aries is very welcome indeed. These subjects are highly intelligent, well-motivated and never leave anything unfinished. They are achievers and will not give up until they reach their goal – which they invariably do. Nothing can stand in the way of Aries Snakes, and they reach the top of whatever tree they climb.

Taurus Snake

In contrast, the sensuous Taurus Snake really can't be bothered with all that hard work. Taurus Snakes have great ability, but they will only do as much as is necessary to acquire the lifestyle they desire, and then they like to sit back and enjoy it. Tremendous sun worshippers, the Taurus Snakes would be quite happy to be on a permanent holiday, providing the accommodation was a five-star hotel with a fabulous restaurant.

Gemini Snake

The Gemini Snake can be a slippery customer. A brilliant brain, linked to a shrewd but amusing tongue, these types can run rings around almost everybody. They can scheme and manipulate if it suits them and pull off all sorts of audacious tricks but having achieved much, they tend to get bored and lose interest, giving up on the brink of great things. This often leads to conflict with business associates who cannot understand such contradictory behaviour. Insane they call it. Suicidal. The Gemini Snake just shrugs and moves on.

Cancer Snake

The Snake born under the sign of Cancer is a more conventional creature. These types will at least do all that is required of them and bring their formidable Snake brains to bear on the task in hand. They are gifted researchers, historians and archaeologists – any career which involves deep concentration and patient study. But the Cancer Snake must take care to mix with cheerful people since left to himself he has a tendency for melancholy. Warmth, laughter, and plenty of rest transforms the Cancer Snake and allows those unique talents to blossom.

Leo Snake

The Leo Snake is a very seductive creature. Beautifully dressed, sparklingly magnetic, few people can take their eyes off these types, and they know it. All Snakes are sensuous, but the Snake born under the sign of Leo is probably the most sensuous of the lot. Never short of admirers, these types are not eager to settle down. Why should they when they're having such a good time? Late in life, the Leo Snake may consent to get married if their partner can offer them a good enough life. If not, these types are quite content to go it alone – probably because they are never truly on their own. They collect willing followers right into old age.

Virgo Snake

The Virgo Snake is another fascinating combination. Highly intuitive and wildly passionate, the Virgo Snake is all elegant understatement on the outside and erotic abandon on the inside. The opposite sex is mesmerised by this intriguing contradiction and just can't stay away. Virgo Snakes can achieve success in their careers if they put their minds to it, but often they are having too much fun flirting and flitting from one lover to the next. Faithfulness is not their strong point, but they are so sexy they get away with murder.

Libra Snake

When you see a top model slinking sinuously down the catwalk, she could very well be a Libra Snake. Snakes born under this sign are the most elegant and stylish of the lot. They may not be conventionally good looking, but they will turn heads wherever they go. These types really understand clothes and could make a plastic bin-liner look glamorous just by putting it on. Somehow, they have the knack of stepping off a transatlantic flight without a crease and driving an open-topped sports car without ruffling their hair. No-one knows quite how they achieve these feats, and Libra Snake isn't telling.

Scorpio Snake

The Snake born under Scorpio is destined to have a complicated life. These types enjoy plots and intrigues, particularly of a romantic nature and spend endless hours devising schemes and planning subterfuge. That ingenious Snake brain is capable of brewing up the most elaborate scams, and there's nothing Scorpio Snake loves more than watching all the parts fall into place. But schemes have a knack of going wrong, and schemers have to change their plans and change them again to cope with each new contingency as it arises. If he's not careful, the Scorpio Snake can become hopelessly embroiled in his own plot.

Sagittarius Snake

Traditionally other signs are wary of the Snake and tend to hold back a little from them without knowing why. When the Snake is born under Sagittarius, however, the subject seems more approachable than most. Sagittarian Snakes sooner or later become recognised for their wisdom and down to earth good sense and people flock to them for advice. Without ever intending to, the Sagittarius Snake could end up as something of a guru attracting eager acolytes desperate to learn more.

Capricorn Snake

The Snake born under Capricorn is more ambitious than the average serpent. These types will reach for the stars and grasp them. Obstacles just melt away when faced with the dual-beam of Capricorn Snake intelligence and quiet persistence. These Snakes are good providers and more dependable than most Snakes. They often end up surrounded by all the trappings of success, but they accomplish this so quietly, no one can quite work out how they managed it.

Aquarius Snake

Another highly intuitive Snake. Independent but people-loving Aquarius endows the serpent with greater social skills than usual. These types attract many friends, and they have the ability to understand just how others are feeling without them having to say a word. These Snakes have particularly enquiring minds, and they can't pass a museum or book shop without going in to browse. Born researchers, they love to dig and delve into whatever subject has taken their fancy, no matter how obscure. Quite often, they discover something valuable by accident.

Pisces Snake

Pisces Snakes tend to live on their nerves even more than most. These types are friendly up to a point, but they hate disagreements and problems and withdraw when things look unpleasant. They are sexy and sensuous and would much prefer a quiet evening with just one special person than a wild party. In the privacy of their bedroom, anything goes, and Pisces Snakes reveal the naughty side of their characters. No one would guess from the understated elegance of their exteriors what an erotic creature the Pisces Snake really is.

Horse

Aries Horse

Overflowing with energy the Aries Horse just can't sit still for long. These types just have to find an outlet for their phenomenal vitality. They are hardworking, hard-playing, and usually highly popular. Less fun-loving signs might be accused of being workaholics but not the Aries Horse. People born under this sign devote enormous amounts of time to their careers but still have so much spare capacity there is plenty left over for their friends. They always do well in their chosen profession.

Taurus Horse

The Taurus Horse can be a trickier creature. Charming yet logical, he has a very good brain and is not afraid to use it. The only problem is that without warning the Taurus Horse can turn from flighty and fun to immensely stubborn and even an earthquake wouldn't shift him from an entrenched position. Yet treated with understanding and patience, the Taurus Horse can be coaxed to produce wonderful achievements.

Gemini Horse

Gemini types are easily bored, and when they are born in the freedom-loving year of the Horse, this trait tends to be accentuated. Unless their attention is caught and held almost instantly, Gemini Horse subjects kick up their heels and gallop off to find more fun elsewhere. For this reason, they often find it difficult to hold on to a job, and they change careers frequently. Yet once they discover a subject about which they can feel passionate, they employ the whole of their considerable talent and will zoom to the top in record time.

Cancer Horse

The Cancer Horse is a lovable creature with a great many friends. These types tend to lack confidence and need a lot of praise and nurturing, but with the right leadership, they will move mountains. Some signs find them difficult to understand because the Cancer Horse loves to be surrounded by a crowd yet needs a lot of alone time too. Misjudge the mood, and the Cancer Horse can seem bafflingly unfriendly. Yet, stay the course, and these subjects become wonderfully loyal friends.

Leo Horse

People born under the star sign of Leo will be the first to admit they like to show off and when they are also born in the year of the Horse, they enjoy showing off all the more. These types love nothing better than strutting around rocking designer outfits while others look on in admiration. They are not so interested in home decor; it's their own personal appearance which counts most. The Leo Horse would much rather invest time and money boosting their image than shoving their earnings into a bank account to gather dust.

Virgo Horse

Virgo types can be a little solemn and over-devoted to duty, but when they are born in the year of the Horse, they are endowed with a welcome streak of equine frivolity. The Virgo Horse loves to party. He will make sure his work is completed first of course, but once the office door clicks shut behind him, the Virgo Horse really knows how to let his hair down.

Libra Horse

The Libra Horse is another true charmer. Friends and acquaintances by the score fill the address books of these types, and their diaries are crammed with appointments. Honest, trustworthy and helpful, other people can't help gravitating to them. Oddly enough, despite their gregarious nature, these types are also very independent. Sometimes too independent for their own good. They are excellent at giving advice to others but find it almost impossible to take advice themselves.

Scorpio Horse

The Scorpio Horse is a real thrill seeker. These types enjoy life's pleasures, particularly passionate pleasures and go all out to attain them. There is no middle road with the Scorpio Horse. These are all or nothing types. They fling themselves into the project of the moment wholeheartedly or not at all. They tend to see things in black and white and believe others are either for them or against them. In serious moments, the Scorpio Horse subscribes to some surprising conspiracy theories, but mostly they keep these ideas to themselves.

Sagittarius Horse

The star sign of Sagittarius is the sign of the Centaur – half-man half-horse – and when these types are born in the year of the Horse, the equine tendencies are so strong they practically have four hooves. Carefree country-lovers these subjects can't bear to be penned in and never feel totally happy until they are out of doors in some wide-open space. They crave fresh air and regular exercise and do best in joint activities. As long as they can spend enough time out of doors, Sagittarius Horses are blessed with glowing good health.

Capricorn Horse

The Capricorn Horse is a canny beast. These types are great savers. They manage to have fun on a shoestring and stash away every spare penny at the same time. They are prepared to work immensely hard provided the pay is good, and they have a remarkable knack of finding just the right job to make the most of their earning power. The Capricorn Horse likes a good time, and he will never be poor.

Aquarius Horse

When Aquarius meets the Horse, it results in a very curious creature. These types admit to enquiring minds; other less charitable signs might call them nosey parkers. Call them what you may, subjects born under this sign need to know and discover. They often become inventors, and they have a weakness for new gadgets and the latest technology. The Aquarius Horse can be wildly impractical and annoy partners by frittering cash away on their latest obsession. They also tend to fill their living space with peculiar objects from junk shops and car boot sales, which they intend to upcycle into useful treasures. Somehow, they seldom get round to finishing the project.

Pisces Horse

Artistic Pisces adds an unusual dimension to the physical Horse, who normally has little time for cultural frills and foibles. These types are great home entertainers and often gifted cooks as well. They invite a group of friends around at the slightest excuse and can conjure delicious snacks and drinks from the most unpromising larders. They adore company and get melancholy if left alone too long.

Goat

Aries Goat

Normally mild and unassuming, the Goat can become almost argumentative when born under the star sign of Aries. Though friendly and very seldom cross, the Aries Goat will suddenly adopt an unexpectedly stubborn position and stick to it unreasonably even when it's obvious he is wrong. Despite this, these types are blessed with sunny natures and are quickly forgiven. They don't bear a grudge and have no idea – after the awkwardness – that anything unpleasant occurred.

Taurus Goat

Like his Aries cousin, the Taurus Goat can turn stubborn too. These types have a very long fuse. Most people would assume they did not have a temper because it is so rarely displayed. But make them truly angry, and they will explode. Small they may be, but a raging Goat can be a fearful sight. On the other hand, these Goats are more likely to have a sweet tooth than their cousins, so if you do upset them, a choccy treat could work wonders in making amends.

Gemini Goat

The Goat born under Gemini is a terrible worrier. These types seem to use their active minds to dream up all the troubles and problems that could result from every single action. Naturally, this renders decision-making almost impossible. They dither and rethink and ponder until finally someone else makes up their mind for them, at which point they are quite happy. In fact, if the Gemini Goat never had to make another decision, she would be a blissfully content creature.

Cancer Goat

Gentle, soft-hearted and kind, the Cancer Goat is a friend to all in need. These types would give their last penny to a homeless beggar in the street, and they always have a shoulder ready should anyone need to cry on it. Yet they can also be surprisingly moody for what appears to be no reason at all, and this characteristic can be baffling to their friends. No point in wasting time asking what's wrong, they find it difficult to explain. Just wait for the clouds to pass.

Leo Goat

The Leo Goat is a very fine specimen. Warm, friendly and more extrovert than her quieter Goat cousins, she seems to have the confidence other Goats often lack. Look more closely though, and you can find all is not quite as it seems. Frequently, that self-assured appearance is merely a well-presented 'front'. Back in the privacy of their own home, the bold Leo Goat can crumble. In truth, these types are easily hurt.

Virgo Goat

Outwardly vague and preoccupied, the Virgo Goat can turn unexpectedly fussy. These types are easy-going, but they can't stand messy homes, mud in their car or sweet wrappers lying around. Yet they would be genuinely surprised if anyone accused them of being pernickety. They believe they are laid back and good-humoured, which they are. Just don't drop chewing gum on their front path, that's all, and take your shoes off at the door.

Libra Goat

The Libra Goat is obliging to the point of self-sacrifice. These types are truly nice people. Generous with their time as well as their possessions. Unfortunately, their good nature is sometimes exploited by the unscrupulous. The Libra Goat will wear itself out in the service of those in distress, will refuse to hear a bad word about anyone and will remain loyal to friends despite the most intense provocation. The Libra Goat lives to please.

Scorpio Goat

Scorpio Goats are among the most strong-willed of all the Goats. They like to go their own way and hate to have others tell them what to do. They don't mind leaving irksome chores and duties to others, but woe betides anyone who tries to interfere with the Scorpio Goat's pet project. At first sight, they may appear preoccupied and have their heads in the clouds, but beneath that vague exterior, their sharp eyes miss very little. Don't underestimate the Scorpio Goat.

Sagittarius Goat

Sagittarius lends an adventurous streak to the normally cautious Goat make-up, and these types tend to take far more risks than their cousins born at other times of the year. While they still enjoy being taken care of, the Sagittarius Goat prefers cosseting on his return from adventures, not instead of them. These types are often good in business and amaze everyone by doing 'extremely well' apparently by accident.

Capricorn Goat

The Capricorn Goat, in contrast, is a very cautious creature. Danger beckons at every turn and security is top of their list of priorities. This Goat can never get to sleep until every door and window has been locked and secured. Should they find themselves staying in a hotel, Capricorn Goats will often drag a chair in front of the bedroom door, just in case. These types are difficult to get to know because it takes a while to win their trust, but once they become friends, they will be loyal forever and despite their caution – or sensible outlook as they'd call it – they can be very successful.

Aquarius Goat

The Aquarius Goat tends to leap about from one high-minded project to the next. These well-meaning types might be manning a soup kitchen one day and devising a scheme to combat climate change the next. Their grand plans seldom come to fruition because they find the practical details so difficult to put into operation but should they link up with an organisational genius they could achieve great things.

Pisces Goat

The Pisces Goat is a very sensitive soul. These types are often highly gifted, and their best course of action is to find someone to take care of them as soon as possible so that they can get on with cultivating their talents. Left to themselves Pisces Goats will neglect their physical needs, failing to cook proper meals or dress warmly in cold weather. With the right guidance, however, they can work wonders.

Monkey

Aries Monkey

These cheeky types have a charm that is quite irresistible. Energetic and mischievous they adore parties and social gatherings of any kind. They crop up on every guest list because they are so entertaining. The Aries Monkey is a font of funny stories and silly jokes but seldom stands still for long. Friends of the Aries Monkey are often frustrated as their popular companion is so in demand it's difficult to pin her down for a catch-up.

Taurus Monkey

The Monkey born under the star sign of Taurus has a little more weight in his character. These types take life a shade more seriously than their delightfully frivolous cousins. Not that the Taurus Monkey is ever a stick-in-the-mud. It's just that business comes before pleasure with these types, although only just, and the business that catches their eye is not necessarily what others would call business. Taurus Monkey is as captivated by creating a useful container out of an old coffee jar as checking out a balance sheet.

Gemini Monkey

The Gemini Monkey Is a true comedian. Incredibly quick-witted, these types only have to open their mouths, and everyone around them is in stitches. If Oscar Wilde was not a Gemini Monkey, he should have been. People born under this sign could easily make a career in the comedy field if they can be bothered to make enough attempts. Truth is they're just as happy entertaining their friends as a theatre full of people.

Cancer Monkey

These types have a gentler side to their characters. Cancer Monkey's love to tinker with machinery and see how things work. They tend to take things to pieces and then forget to put them together again. They are easily hurt, however, if someone complains about this trait. They genuinely intend to put things right. It is just that, somehow, they never manage to get round to it, and they never realise that this is a trait they repeat over and over again.

Leo Monkey

The Leo Monkey is a highly adaptable creature. He can be all things to all men while still retaining his own unique personality. Popular, amusing and fond of practical jokes these types are welcome wherever they go. They can sometimes get rather carried away with the sound of their own voices and end up being rather tactless, but such is their charm that everyone forgives them. Occasionally, a practical joke can go too far, but kind-hearted Leo Monkey is horrified if anyone feels hurt, and instantly apologises.

Virgo Monkey

The Virgo Monkey could be a great inventor. The Monkey's natural ingenuity blends with Virgo's patience and fussiness over detail to create a character with the ideas to discover something new and the tenacity to carry on until it is perfected. If they could curb their impulse to rush on to the next brilliant idea when the last is complete, and turned their intention instead to marketing, they could make a fortune.

Libra Monkey

The Monkey born under the sign of Libra is actually a force to be reckoned with though no-one would ever guess it. These types are lovable and fun and have a knack of getting other people to do what they want without even realising they've been talked into it. In fact, Libran Monkeys are first-class manipulators but so skilled at their craft that nobody minds. These types could get away with murder.

Scorpio Monkey

Normally, the Monkey is a real chatterbox, but when Scorpio is added to the mix, you have a primate with the unusual gift of discretion right alongside his natural loquaciousness. These types will happily gossip all day long, but if they need to keep a secret, they are able to do so, to the grave if necessary. Scorpio Monkey could be an actor or a spy – and play each role to perfection. 007 could well have been a Scorpio Monkey.

Sagittarius Monkey

These flexible, amorous, adventure-loving Monkeys add zing to any gathering. These are the guests with the mad-cap ideas who want to jump fully clothed into the swimming pool at midnight and think it terrific fun to see in the New Year on top of Ben Nevis. It's difficult to keep up with the Sagittarius Monkey, but it's certainly fun to try.

Capricorn Monkey

Capricorn Monkeys have their serious side, but they are also flirty types. These are the subjects who charm with ease and tease and joke their conquests into bed. The trouble is Capricorn Monkey often promises more than is deliverable. These types tire more easily than they realise, and can't always put their exciting schemes into action. This rarely stops them trying, of course.

Aquarius Monkey

The Aquarius Monkey is a particularly inventive creature and employs his considerable intellect in trying to discover new ways to save the world. These types often have a hard time in their early years as it takes them decades to realise that not everyone sees the importance of their passions as they do. But, once they understand a different approach is needed, they go on to accomplish much in later life.

Pisces Monkey

The Pisces Monkey can be a puzzling creature. These types are dreamy and amusing one minute and irritable and quick-tempered the next. They can go with the flow so far and then suddenly wonder why no-one can keep up with them when they decide to get a move on. They tend to lack quite so much humour when the joke is on themselves, but most of the time they are agreeable companions.

Rooster

Aries Rooster

Stand well back when confronted with an Aries Rooster. These types are one hundred percent go-getter, and nothing will stand in their way. Aries Rooster can excel at anything to which he puts his mind, and as he frequently puts his mind to business matters, he's likely to end up a billionaire. Think scarlet sports cars, ostentatious homes, and a personal helicopter or two – the owner is bound to be an Aries Rooster.

Taurus Rooster

The Taurus Rooster has a heart of gold but can come over as a bit of a bossy boots, particularly in financial matters. These types believe they have a unique understanding of money and accounts and are forever trying to get more sloppy signs to sharpen up in this department. Even if their manner rankles, it's worth listening to their advice. Annoyingly, they are often right.

Gemini Rooster

The Rooster born under the sign of Gemini would make a terrific private detective were it not for the fact that Roosters find it almost impossible to blend into the background. Gemini Roosters love to find out what's going on and have an uncanny ability to stumble on the one thing you don't wish them to know. They mean no harm, however, and once they find a suitable outlet for their talents, they will go far.

Cancer Rooster

The Rooster born under the sign of Cancer is often a fine-looking creature and knows it. These types are secretly rather vain and behind the scenes take great pains with their appearance. They would die rather than admit it, however, and like to give the impression that their wonderful style is no more than a happy accident. Though they cultivate a relaxed, easy-going manner, a bad hair day or a splash of mud on their new suede boots is enough to send them into a major sulk for hours.

Leo Rooster

Not everyone takes to the Leo Rooster. The Lion is a naturally proud, extrovert sign and when allied to the strutting Rooster, there is a danger of these types ending up as bossy exhibitionists. Yet they really have the kindest of hearts and will leap from their pedestals in an instant to comfort someone who seems upset. A word of warning – they should avoid excessive alcohol as these types can get merry on a sniff of a cider apple.

Virgo Rooster

The Virgo Rooster is a hardworking, dedicated creature, devoted to family, but in an undemonstrative way. Wind this bird up at your peril, however. These types have little sense of humour when it comes to taking a joke, and they will hold a grudge for months if they feel someone has made them look foolish. They hate to be laughed at.

Libra Rooster

The Libra Rooster likes to look good, have a fine home and share his considerable assets with his closest friends. These types enjoy admiration, but they are more subtle than Leo Roosters and don't demand it quite so openly. Libra Rooster is quite happy to give but does expect gratitude in return.

Scorpio Rooster

The Scorpio Rooster is a heroic creature. These types will defend a position to the death. In days of old, many a Scorpio Rooster will have got involved in a duel because these types cannot endure insults, will fight aggression with aggression and will not back down under any circumstances. Foolhardy they may appear, but there is something admirable about them nevertheless.

Sagittarius Rooster

The Sagittarius Rooster tends to be a little excitable and rash. These types are bold and brash and ready for anything. They love to travel and are desperate to see what's over the next hill and around the next bend. Born explorers' they never want to tread the conventional travel path. Let others holiday in Marbella if they wish. Sagittarius Rooster prefers a walking tour of Tibet.

Capricorn Rooster

Capricorn brings a steadying quality to the impulsive Rooster. These types like to achieve, consolidate, and then build again. They believe they are amassing a fortune for their family and they usually do. However, sometimes, their families would prefer a little less security and more attention. Best not to mention it to Capricorn Rooster though – this Rooster is likely to feel hurt and offended.

Aquarius Rooster

The Aquarius Rooster is frequently misunderstood. These types mean well but they tend to be impulsive and speak before they think, accidentally offending others when they do so. In fact, the Aquarius Rooster is a sensitive creature beneath that brash exterior and is easily hurt. If they can learn to count to ten before saying anything controversial, and maybe rephrase, they'd be amazed at how successful they'd become.

Pisces Rooster

The Pisces Rooster has a secret fear. He is terrified that one day he will be terribly poor. These types save hard to stave off that dreadful fate and will only feel totally relaxed when they have a huge nest egg behind them. Despite this, they manage to fall in and out of love regularly and often end up delighting their partners with the wonderful lifestyle they can create.

Dog

Aries Dog

The Aries Dog is a friendly type. Extrovert and sociable these subjects like a lively career and cheerful home life. They are not excessively materialistic, but they tend to make headway in the world without trying too hard. Aries Dog likes to get things done and will bound from one task to the next with energy and enthusiasm.

Taurus Dog

The Dog born under the star sign of Taurus is the most dependable creature in the world. Their word really is their bond, and they will never break a promise while there is breath in their body. They tend to be ultra-conservative with a small 'c'. The men are inclined to be chauvinists, and the women usually hold traditional views. They really do prefer to make their home and family their priority. They are loyal and kind, and people instinctively trust them.

Gemini Dog

The Gemini Dog, in contrast, while never actually dishonest, can be a bit of a sly fox when necessary. The quickest of all Dogs, the Gemini breed gets impatient when the going gets slow and resorts to the odd trick to speed things along. Nevertheless, these types are truthful and honest in their own way and have a knack of falling on their feet... whatever happens.

Cancer Dog

The Cancer Dog was born to be in a settled relationship. These types are never totally happy until they've found their true love and built a cosy home to snuggle up in together. Cancer Dog is not overly concerned with a career. As long as these types earn enough to pay the mortgage and buy life's essentials, they are happy. The right companionship is what they crave. With the perfect partner by their side, they are truly content.

Leo Dog

If Leo Dogs really did have four legs, chances are they would be police dogs. These types are sticklers for law and order. They will not tolerate injustice and will seek out wrongdoers and plague them until they change their ways. Woe betide any workmate who is pilfering pens, making free with office coffee or fiddling expenses. The Leo Dog will force them to own up and make amends. Should you be a victim of injustice, however, Leo Dog will zoom to your aid.

Virgo Dog

The Virgo Dog tends to be a great worrier. A born perfectionist, Virgo Dog agonises over every detail and loses sleep if he suspects he has performed any task badly. These types are very clever and can achieve great things, but too often they fail to enjoy their success because they are too busy worrying they might have made a mistake. The crazy thing is, they very seldom do.

Libra Dog

The Libra Dog believes in 'live and let live'. A laid back, tolerant fellow, Libra Dog likes to lie in the sun and not interfere with anyone. Let sleeping dogs lie is definitely her motto. She will agree to almost anything for a quiet life. Yet it's unwise to push her too far. When there's no alternative, this particular hound can produce a very loud bark.

Scorpio Dog

The Scorpio Dog is as loyal and trustworthy as other canines, but more difficult to get to know. Beneath that amiable exterior is a very suspicious heart. These types don't quite understand why they are so wary of others, but it takes them a long time to learn to trust. Perhaps they are afraid of getting hurt. The idea of marriage fills them with terror, and it takes a very patient partner to get them to the altar. Once married, however, they will be faithful and true.

Sagittarius Dog

The Sagittarius Dog is inexhaustible. These cheerful types are always raring to go and quite happy to join in with any adventure. They love to be part of the gang and are perfectly willing to follow someone else's lead. They don't mind if their ideas are not always accepted; they just like being involved. These types work splendidly in teams and can achieve great things in a group.

Capricorn Dog

The Capricorn Dog is a very caring type. These subjects are happy so long as their loved ones are happy, but they greatly fear that a friend or family member might fall ill. This concern, probably kept secret, gives them real anxiety and should a loved one show worrying symptoms, the Capricorn Dog will suffer sleepless nights until the problem is resolved. When they are not urging their families to keep warm and put on an extra vest, these types are likely to be out and about helping others less fortunate than themselves.

Aquarius Dog

The Aquarius Dog, when young, spends a great deal of time searching for a worthy cause to which they can become devoted. Since there are so many worthy causes from which to choose these types can suffer much heartache as they struggle to pick the right one. When – at last – a niche is found, however, the Aquarius Dog will settle down to a truly contented life of quiet satisfaction. These types need to serve and feel that they are improving life for others. This is their path to happiness.

Pisces Dog

Like the Aquarius breed, the Pisces Dog often has a number of false starts early in life although these are more likely to be of a romantic rather than philanthropic nature. The Pisces Dog wants to find a soulmate but is not averse to exploring a few cul-de-sacs on the way. These types are not promiscuous, however, and when they do find Mr or Miss Right, they are blissfully happy to settle down.

Pig

Aries Pig

The Aries Pig always seems to wear a smile on its face and no wonder. Everything seems to go right for these cheerful types, and they scarcely seem to have to lift a finger to make things fall perfectly into place. In fact, of course, their good luck is the result of sheer hard work, but the Aries Pig has a knack of making work look like play so that nobody realises the effort Pig is putting in.

Taurus Pig

Most Pigs are happy, but the Taurus Pigs really seem quite blissful most of the time. One of their favourite occupations is eating, and they delight in dreaming up sumptuous menus and then creating them for the enjoyment of themselves and their friends. For this reason, Taurus Pigs have a tendency to put on weight. Despite the time they devote to their hobby, however, Taurus Pigs usually do well in their career. Many gifted designers are born under this sign.

Gemini Pig

The Gemini Pig has a brilliant business brain gift-wrapped in a charming, happy go lucky personality. These types usually zoom straight to the top of their chosen tree, but they manage to do so smoothly and easily without ruffling too many feathers on the way. They are popular with their workmates, and later their employees, and nobody can figure out how quite such a nice, down to earth type has ended up in such a position of authority.

Cancer Pig

The Cancer Pig likes to give the impression of being a very hard-working type. She is hard working, of course, but perhaps not quite as excessively as she likes others to believe. Secretly, the Cancer Pig makes sure there's plenty of time to spare for fun and indulgence. To the outside world, however, Pig pretends to be constantly slaving away and likes to get regular appreciation for these efforts.

Leo Pig

The Leo Pig is delightful company. Friendly, amusing and very warm and approachable. These types do however have a tremendously lazy streak. Left to themselves, they would not rise till noon, and they prefer someone else to do all the cleaning and cooking. The Leo Pig has to be nagged to make an effort, but when these types do so, they can achieve impressive results.

Virgo Pig

The Virgo Pig, in contrast, is a highly conscientious creature. These types can't abide laziness, and while they are normally kindly, helpful souls who gladly assist others, they will not lift a finger to aid someone who has brought his problems on himself through slovenliness. The Virgo Pig is a clean, contented type who usually achieves a happy life.

Libra Pig

The creative Libra Pig is always dreaming up new ways to improve their home. These types love to be surrounded by beautiful and comfortable things but seldom get round to completing their ideas because they are having such a good time in other ways. This is probably just as well because the minute they decide on one colour scheme, they suddenly see something that might work better. A permanent work in progress is probably the best option.

Scorpio Pig

The Scorpio Pig usually goes far. The amiable Pig boosted by powerful, almost psychic Scorpio can seem turbo-charged at times. These types keep their own counsel more than their chatty cousins, and this often stands them in good stead in business. They can be a little too cautious at times, but they rarely make mistakes.

Sagittarius Pig

Eat, drink and be merry is the motto of the Sagittarius Pig. These types have the intelligence to go far in their careers but, in truth, they would rather party. They love to dress up, get together with a bunch of friends and laugh and dance until dawn. Sagittarius Pig hates to be alone for long, so is always off in search of company.

Capricorn Pig

Pigs are normally broad-minded types, but the Capricorn Pig is a little more staid than his cousins. Nevertheless, being able to narrow their vision gives these types the ability to channel their concentration totally onto the subject in hand, a gift which is vital to success in many professions. For this reason, Capricorn Pigs often make a name for themselves in their chosen career.

Aquarius Pig

Honest, straightforward and popular Aquarius Pigs have more friends than they can count. Always good-humoured and cheerful these types gravitate to those in need and do whatever they can to help. The Aquarius Pig gives copiously to charity and frequently wishes to do more. These types tend to have their heads in the clouds most of the time and for this reason, tend not to give their careers or finances the attention they should. But since worldly success means little to the Aquarius Pig, this hardly matters.

Pisces Pig

The Pisces Pig is a particularly sweet-natured creature. These types are real dreamers. They float around in a world of their own, and people tend to make allowances for them. Yet, from time to time, the Pisces Pig drifts in from his other planet to startle everyone with a stunningly brilliant idea. There is more to the Pisces Pig than meets the eye.

Rat

Aries Rat

Fiery Aries adds more than usual urgency to the sociable Rat. While these types enjoy company, they also tend to be impatient and can get quite bad-tempered and aggressive with anyone who seems to waste their time. Aries Rats do not suffer fools and will stomp off on their own if someone annoys them. In fact, this is the best thing all round. Aries Rats hate to admit it, but they benefit from a little solitude which enables them to calm down and recharge their batteries. Happily, as quickly as these types flare up, they just as quickly cool off again.

Taurus Rat

When Taurus, renowned for a love of luxury and the finer things in life, is born in a comfort-loving Rat year, a true gourmet and bon viveur has entered the world. The Taurus effect enhances the sensuous parts of the Rat personality and lifts them to new heights. Good food is absolutely essential to these types. They don't eat to live; they really do live to eat. Many excellent chefs are born under this sign, and even those folks who don't make catering their career are likely to be outstanding home cooks. Dinner parties thrown by Taurus Rats are memorable affairs. The only drawback with these types is that they can become a little pernickety and overly fussy about details. They also have to watch their weight.

Gemini Rat

While Taurus accentuates the Rat's love of good living, Gemini heightens the Rat's already well-developed social skills. That crowd chuckling and laughing around the witty type in the corner are bound to be listening to a Gemini Rat. Amusing, quick-thinking, and never lost for words, the only things likely to drive Gemini Rats away are bores and undue seriousness. Gemini Rats prefer light, entertaining conversation and head for the hills when things get too heavy. Delightful as they always are however, it is difficult to capture the attention of a Gemini Rat for long. These types love to circulate. They make an entrance and then move on to pastures new. Pinning them down never works. They simply lose interest and with it that famous sparkle.

Cancer Rat

Cancer makes the Rat a little more sensitive and easily hurt than usual. These types are emotional and loving but sometimes come across as martyrs. They work hard but tend to feel, often without good cause, their efforts are not as well appreciated as they should be. Cancer Rats frequently suspect they are being taken for granted at home and at work, but their love of company prevents them from making too big a fuss. Rats are naturally gifted business people, and the Cancer Rat has a particularly good head for financial affairs. These types enjoy working with others, and they are especially well suited to partnerships. However, don't expect the sensitive, feeling Cancer Rat to be a pushover. These types can be surprisingly demanding at work and will not tolerate any laziness on the part of employees.

Leo Rat

Leo Rats usually get to the top. Few people can resist them. The combination of Rat sociability, business acumen and ambition, coupled with extrovert Leo's rather, shall we say, 'pushy', qualities and flair for leadership can't help but power these types to the top of whatever tree they happen to choose to climb. Along the way, however, they may irritate those few less gifted souls who fail to fall under their spell. Such doubters may complain that Leo Rat hogs the limelight and tends to become overbearing at times but since hardly anyone else seems to notice, why should Leo Rat care?

Virgo Rat

As we have already seen, the delightful Rat does have a stingy streak in his make-up, and when the astrological sign of Virgo is added to the mix, this characteristic tends to widen. At best, Virgo Rats are terrific savers and do wonders with their investments. The Rat tendency to squander money on unwise bargains is almost entirely absent in these types, and they often end up seriously rich. At worst, however, in negative types, Virgo Rats can be real Scrooges, grating the last sliver of soap to save on washing powder, sitting in the dark to conserve electricity and attempting their own shoe repairs with stick-on soles, even when they have plenty of money in the bank. Virgo Rats are brilliant at detail; but in negative types, they put this gift to poor use spending far too long on money-saving schemes when they would do much better to look for ways of expanding their income.

Libra Rat

The Libra Rat adores company even more than most. In fact, these types are seldom alone. They have dozens of friends, their phones never stop ringing, and most evenings the Libra Rat is entertaining. Libra Rat enjoys civilised gatherings rather than wild parties and friends will be treated to beautiful music, exquisite food and a supremely comfortable home. These types really can charm the birds off the trees, not with the brilliant repartee of the Gemini Rat but with a warmth and low-key humour all their own. These types do tend to be a touch lazier than the usual Rat and their weakness for bargains, particularly in the areas of art and fashion, is more pronounced, but their charm is so strong that partners forgive them for overspending.

Scorpio Rat

It's often said that Rats would make good journalists or detectives because beneath that expansive surface is a highly observant brain. Well the best of them all would be the Rat born under Scorpio. A veritable

Sherlock Holmes of a Rat if you wish to be flattering, or a real nosey parker if you don't. These types are endlessly curious. They want to know everything that's going on, who is doing what with whom where and for how long. They may not have any particular use for the information they gather, but they just can't help gathering it all the same. Scorpio Rats often have psychic powers though they may not be aware of this and these powers aid them in their 'research'. Unlike other Rats, those born under Scorpio prefer their own company and like to work alone. When they manage to combine their curiosity and talent for digging out information, there is almost no limit to what they can achieve with their career

Sagittarius Rat

Traditionally Rats have many friends, but the Sagittarius Rat has the not so welcome distinction of collecting a few enemies along the way as well. The Sagittarius Rat finds this quite extraordinary as he never intends to upset anyone. It's just that these types can be forthright to the point of rudeness and an affable nature can only compensate so far. These types are amicable and warm, but when they speak their minds, some people never forgive them. Despite this tendency, Sagittarius Rats have a knack for accumulating money and plough it back into their business to good effect. They manage to be generous, and a bit mean at the same time, which baffles their friends, but those that have not been offended by Sagittarius Rat's tactless tongue tend to stay loyal forever.

Capricorn Rat

Rats are naturally high achievers, but perhaps the highest achiever of them all is likely to be born under the sign of Capricorn. These types are not loud and brilliant like Leo Rats. They tend to be quietly ambitious. They keep in the background, watching what needs to be done, astutely judging who counts and who does not, and then when they are absolutely sure they are on solid ground, they move in. After such preparation, they are unlikely to make a mistake, but if they do they blame themselves, they are bitterly angry, and they resolve never to repeat their stupidity. Reckless these types are not, but their methods produce good results, and they make steady progress towards their goals.

Aquarius Rat

All Rats are blessed with good brains, but few of them think of themselves as intellectuals. The exceptions are the Rats born under the sign of Aquarius. While being friendly and sociable, the Aquarian Rat also needs time alone to think things through and to study the latest subject that has aroused his interest. Perhaps not so adept at business as most Rats, those born under the sign of Aquarius make up for any deficiency in this department by teeming with good ideas. They are intuitive, very hard working and love to be involved in 'people' projects.

Pisces Rat

Pisces Rats tend to be quieter than their more flamboyant brothers and sisters. They are not drawn to the limelight, and they are not so interested in business as other Rats. In fact, working for other people has little appeal for them, although this is what they often end up doing through want of thinking up a better idea. Should a more enterprising Pisces Rat decide to put his mind to business, however, he will often end up self-employed which suits him extremely well. Having taken the plunge, many a self-employed Pisces Rat surprises himself by doing very well indeed. These types can be amazingly shrewd and intuitive, and once these powers are harnessed to the right career, they progress in leaps and bounds. Pisces Rats tend to do well in spite of themselves.

Ox

Aries Ox

Dynamic Aries brings the Ox a very welcome blast of fire and urgency to stir those methodical bones into faster action. This is a fortunate combination because when the steadfast, industrious, patient qualities of the Ox are combined with quickness of mind and a definite purpose, very little can stand in the way of this subject's progress. Aries Oxen do particularly well in careers where enormous discipline combined with flair and intelligence is required. Many writers are born under this sign as are college lecturers, historical researchers and archaeologists.

Taurus Ox

Oxen are notoriously stubborn creatures but combine them with Taurus the bull and this trait is doubled if not quadrupled. It is not a good idea to box these types into a corner because they will take a stand and refuse to budge even if the house is on fire. Taurean Oxen really will cut off their noses to spite their faces if they feel they have to. Fall out with them and stop talking, and the chances are that the feud will continue to the grave. Yet despite this tendency, Oxen born under the sign of Taurus are not unfriendly types. They are utterly reliable and totally loyal. Family and friends trust them completely. They might be a bit old fashioned and inflexible, but they are lovable too.

Gemini Ox

Chatty Gemini transforms the normally taciturn Ox into a beast which is almost loquacious, at least by the normal standards of these strong silent types. They might even be confident enough to attempt a few jokes, and though humour is not the Oxen's strongpoint, the Gemini Ox can usually produce something respectably amusing if not sidesplittingly funny. Oddly enough, should the Ox set his mind to it and apply his awesome hard work and patience to the subject of humour he might even make a career of it. Some Gemini Oxen have even become accomplished comedians – not simply through natural talent but through sheer hard work and perseverance. More frequently, however, the combination of Gemini with the Ox produces a 'poor man's lawyer' – a highly opinionated individual who can see what's wrong with the government and the legal system and loves to put the world to rights at every opportunity.

Cancer Ox

Oxen born under the sign of Cancer can go very far indeed, not through the application of brainpower although they are by no means unintelligent, but through the skills they have at their fingertips. These subjects are the craftsmen of the universe. Diligent, painstaking, and precise, they are incapable of bodging any practical task they undertake. They will spend hours and hours honing whatever craft has taken their fancy until they reach what looks to others like the peak of perfection. The Cancer Ox won't accept this of course. He can detect the minutest flaw in his own handiwork, but when he is finally forced to hand it over, everyone else is delighted with his efforts. Many artists, potters and sculptors are born under this sign.

Leo Ox

When the Lion of Leo meets the enormous strength of the Ox, the result is a formidable individual, indeed. Annoy or mock these powerful types at your peril. And anyone who dares to pick a fight with the Lion-Ox is likely to come out of it very badly. Most of the time, however, Leo is a friendly lion bringing confidence and a more relaxed attitude to the unbending Ox. These types are more broad-minded and open-hearted than the usual Oxen. They have been known to enjoy parties and once tempted into the limelight they may even find it's not as bad as they feared. In fact, secretly, they're having a ball.

Virgo Ox

Oxen born under the sign of Virgo tend to be very caring types. Though they show their feelings in practical ways and shun sloppy, emotional displays you can rely on an Ox born under Virgo to comfort the sick, help the old folk and notice if anyone in the neighbourhood needs assistance. Florence Nightingale could have been a Virgo Ox. The unsentimental but immensely useful and humane work she did for her sick soldiers is typical of these types. They make excellent nurses and careworkers, forever plumping pillows, smoothing sheets and knowing just the right touches to bring comfort where it is needed. On a personal level, these subjects are inclined to be critical and easily irritated by the small failings of others, but their bark is worse than their bite. Their kindness shines through.

Libra Ox

Generally speaking, the down to earth Ox has little time for putting on the charm. As far as Ox is concerned, people either like you or they don't, and it's not worth worrying about it either way. There's no point in wasting valuable time trying to bend your personality to accommodate the whims of others. Yet when the Ox is born under the sign of Libra, this trait is modified somewhat. Libra people just can't help having charm even if they are Oxen and therefore express that charm more brusquely than usual. The Libran Ox glides effortlessly through life, pleasing others without even realising it. These types are sympathetic and like to help those in need wherever possible. Try to take advantage of their good nature or trick them with an untrue sob story, though, and they will never forgive you.

Scorpio Ox

The typical Ox is notoriously difficult to get to know, and when that Ox happens to be born under the secretive sign of Scorpio, you might as well give up and go home. You'll learn nothing from this creature unless he has some special reason for telling you. Stubborn and silent, these types are very deep indeed; they care nothing for the opinions of others and follow their own impenetrable hearts come what may. However, win the love of one of these unique subjects, and you have a very rare prize indeed. You will unlock a devotion and passion that you have probably never experienced before and will probably never experience again. This is a strangely compelling combination.

Sagittarius Ox

The Ox born under Sagittarius is a more carefree type than his brothers and sisters. Something of the free spirit of the horse touches these subjects, and while there is no chance of them kicking up their heels or doing anything remotely irresponsible, they at least understand these temptations in others and take a more relaxed view of life. The Ox born under Sagittarius is ambitious but independent. These types don't like to be told what to do and are probably more suited to being self-employed than working for others. They are more easy-going than a lot of Oxen and for this reason attract a wider range of friends. Like their Gemini cousins, they might even hazard a joke from time to time. All in all, the Ox born under Sagittarius gets more fun out of life.

Capricorn Ox

Unlike his Sagittarian brother, the Ox born under Capricorn takes himself and life very seriously indeed. These types usually do very well in material terms and often end up in positions of authority; yet if they're not careful, they can look burned out. With good reason. Capricorn Oxen have never learned how to relax, and they see life as a struggle; consequently, for them, it is. Yet they have much to be glad for. They are great savers for a rainy day, and so they never have to worry about unpaid bills, their capacity for hard work is so enormous they can hardly help but achieve a great deal, and before very long they find themselves well off and regarded with respect by everyone in the community. If these types could only manage to unwind, be gentle with themselves and enjoy their success, they could be very happy indeed.

Aquarius Ox

The Ox has never been a flashy sign. These types believe actions speak louder than words, and they like to beaver away without drawing attention to themselves. When this trait is coupled with the slightly introverted though idealistic nature of Aquarius, you get a quiet, complex character who prefers to work behind the scenes and turns modest when the limelight is switched on. Never known for his verbal dexterity, the Ox born under Aquarius can suddenly turn into a persuasive orator when a humanitarian cause sparks unexpected passion. These types make loyal, faithful companions to those who take the trouble to understand them and their intelligence and dogged persistence makes them invaluable as researchers, political assistants and private secretaries.

Pisces Ox

Few Oxen can be described as fey, changeable creatures but those that come the closest will be found under the sign of Pisces. Pisces brings an emotional, artistic quality to the steadfast Ox. These types are loving, faithful and true, yet it is often difficult to guess what they are thinking. Of all the Ox family, Pisces Oxen are likely to be the most moody and yet in many ways also the most creative. The Ox input lends strength and stamina to more delicate Pisces constitutions, enabling them to accomplish far more than other Pisces subjects. Just leave them alone until they're ready to face the world.

Tiger

Aries Tiger

Another combination which could be potentially explosive but, in this case, energetic Aries adds force and power to the Tiger's humanitarian instincts while the Tiger's unworldly nature curbs Aries materialistic streak. These types really could change the world for the better if they put their minds to it. They are kind and thoughtful, and while they might be impatient at times, they quickly regret any harsh words spoken in the heat of the moment.

Taurus Tiger

Taurus Tigers are tremendous achievers. The strength of the zodiac bull added to the fire of the Tiger produces a truly formidable individual who can do almost anything to which he sets his mind. These types often end up making a great deal of money. They have to work hard for all their gains, but this doesn't worry them at all. They also take a great deal of pleasure in spending their hard-earned cash. They like to share what they've got, and this gives them such childish joy that no-one begrudges them their good fortune.

Gemini Tiger

The quicksilver mind of Gemini adds zing and extra flexibility to the Tiger's powerful individualism. These Tigers are blessed with minds which overflow with brilliant ideas. They are creative and often artistic too, so they're capable of wonderful achievements. Their only drawback is that they possess almost too much of a good thing. They have so many ideas that they tend to zoom off at a tangent onto a new task before they have completed the one on which they were working.

Cancer Tiger

These Tigers are immensely clever but a little more retiring than the usual bold, brave terror of the jungle. No Tiger is timid, but Cancer has the effect of quietening the more reckless excesses of the Tiger and allowing a little caution to creep into the blend. They still like a challenge but will opt for something a little less physically demanding than other Tigers. These types are more able to fit into society and tolerate authority better than other Tigers, and for this reason they often do well in their careers.

Leo Tiger

What would you get if you crossed a lion with a tiger? A very wild beast indeed. Some sort of striped wonder of the world no doubt! Leo Tigers certainly make their mark. Tigers are big, beautiful, fearless personalities who crave the limelight and love to be noticed. They believe in doing good deeds, but they like to be noticed doing them. These are not the types of which anonymous benefactors are made. When the Leo Tiger raises money for charity, he likes to make sure the world's press are gathered to record the occasion if at all possible. Yet his heart's in the right place. Let these Tigers have their share of praise, and they will work wonders for others.

Virgo Tiger

The Virgo Tiger is quite a different beast. Virgo accentuates the Tiger's already well-developed sense of justice. These types cannot rest until wrongdoers have got their just deserts. They often go into professions involving the law and the police force. They are immensely self-disciplined and have very high standards. Totally trustworthy and effective, they can sometimes be a little difficult to live with. They are not unkind; it's just that they expect everyone else to be as perfect as they are themselves. Yet Virgo adds attention-to-detail to Tiger's passion to change the world, and the combination creates a character who really could make a lasting difference.

Libra Tiger

Laidback Libra brings quite a different quality to the Tiger. Tiger's intensity is softened by pure Libra charm, and the result is a Tiger of unrivalled compassion and magnetism. Libra Tigers often end up in the caring professions where people flock to them with relief. These Tigers want to help, and Libra gives them the ability to understand just what people need and when. You'd never catch a Libra Tiger helping an old lady across the road who didn't wish to go. Libra Tiger would realise at once that the woman was waiting for a bus, would stand with her to keep her company, help her on when the vehicle arrived and make sure the driver put her off at the right stop. No wonder these Tigers are so well-loved wherever they go.

Scorpio Tiger

Crossing a Scorpion with a Tiger is a very tricky proposition. These types mean well, but they are often misunderstood. Scorpio brings a tremendous depth of feeling to the Tiger's reforming instincts, but this sometimes causes them to put tremendous effort into the wrong causes with alarming results. These types can be very quick-tempered, and they may nurse a grudge for a long time. They never forgive disloyalty, and they never forget. It would be a serious mistake to make an enemy of a Scorpio Tiger – but once this individual becomes a friend, they'll be loyal for life.

Sagittarius Tiger

Another charmer, the Sagittarius Tiger is nevertheless likely to hit the road at the slightest opportunity. These types are wanderers, and no matter how much they seem to enjoy company, they enjoy moving on even more. They can't bear working for other people and do far better being self-employed. The travel industry would suit them perfectly. Impossible to cage in or pin down – don't even try – the only way to have a happy relationship with a Sagittarius Tiger is to make them feel free at all times.

Capricorn Tiger

Steady Capricorn lends a prudent touch to the impulsive Tiger, and these types are the Tigers most likely to stop and think before rushing off to save the rain forest. They still enjoy improving the world, but they check travel arrangements, make sure they have got sufficient funds and do a bit of research online first. These are not party animals. While they enjoy company, they prefer serious discussion to frivolous small talk and much as they enjoy travel, they appreciate the comfort of home. These Tigers like to develop their theories from the depths of their favourite armchair beside their own cosy hearth.

Aquarius Tiger

When idealistic Aquarius meets idealistic Tiger, you have to hang onto that long tiger tail to keep these subjects, feet on the ground. These types really do have their heads in the clouds and are totally unpredictable. Once a worthwhile cause presents itself, they will rush off immediately without a thought to the consequences. Convention is of no interest to them. They couldn't care less what other people think. They go through life guided entirely by a strong inner sense of right and wrong. If it's right, they know it without a shadow of a doubt; if it's wrong, they will not do it no matter what anyone says. This attitude can get them into a lot of trouble, but other signs sneakily admire their courage. People may not agree with Aquarius Tiger, but no one can doubt his integrity.

Pisces Tiger

One of Tiger's failings is a tendency to be indecisive without warning, and this trait is heightened in Pisces Tigers. These types are anxious to do the right thing; it's just that sometimes it's very difficult to know what that right thing is. There are so many alternatives. Pisces Tiger is kind and gentle and apt to get sentimental at times. They want to save the world, but they'd like someone alongside to help them – though not too many. Despite their indecision, they usually end up heading in the right direction in the end. Yet, even when they've achieved a great deal, they still agonise over whether they could have done even more.

Rabbit

Aries Rabbit

This is a very dynamic Rabbit. When powerful Aries injects a streak of energy into that cultured Rabbit personality, the result is a wonderfully clever individual who glides effortlessly to success. Although at times Aries Rabbit has an attack of over-cautiousness, these types are usually bolder than the average bunny and achieve much where other Rabbits might run away. Occasionally, these Rabbits will even take a gamble, and this is worthwhile as it usually pays off for them.

Taurus Rabbit

The Taurus Rabbit really does feel his home is his castle. He is not unduly interested in his career, but he is likely to turn his home into an art form. Brilliant entertainers, these types guarantee their lucky guests will enjoy all the creature comforts possible. They often marry later in life than average, but when they do, they work at the relationship. Providing they choose another home bird, they are likely to be very happy.

Gemini Rabbit

All Rabbits are natural diplomats, but the Gemini Rabbit really is the star of them all. So skilled a communicator is this creature, so expert at people management that a career in the diplomatic service, politics, psychology or even advertising is an option. Never lost for words, these types can persuade anyone to do almost anything. As a result, they are usually very successful. Once they harness their enviable skills to a worthwhile career, they can go far.

Cancer Rabbit

Cancer Rabbits are gentle, kindly souls. They like to be surrounded by pleasant company and prefer to have few demands put upon them. They don't really take to business life and find many professions too abrasive. On the other hand, they find working for themselves too stressful a venture to be considered seriously. They are happiest in a peaceful, routine environment where they can make steady progress, but really their hearts are at home. Home is where they express themselves.

Leo Rabbit

Leo Rabbits, on the other hand, are usually very popular with a wide circle of friends. Extrovert Leo gives Rabbit a strong dose of confidence and flair, and when these qualities are added to Rabbit's people skills, a radiant, magnetic individual is born. Leo Rabbits adore parties where they shine. They are always elegant and beautifully turned out and have a knack of putting others at their ease. These Rabbits climb the ladder of success very quickly.

Virgo Rabbit

Virgo Rabbits have a lot on their minds. The natural cautiousness of the Rabbit is heightened by the same quality in Virgo, and these Rabbits tend to be born worriers. They are masters of detail but, unfortunately, this often leads them to make mountains out of molehills. They are very talented creatures but too often fail to make the best use of their gifts because they spend so much time worrying about all the things that could go wrong. If they can learn to relax and take the odd risk now and then, they will go far.

Libra Rabbit

Art-loving Libra blends easily into the cultured sign of the Rabbit. These types love to learn more about beautiful things, and they like to share their knowledge with others. They are so good with people that they can convey information effortlessly and make the dullest subject sound interesting. These types are often gifted teachers and lecturers though they would find difficult inner-city schools too traumatic. Give these types willing and interested pupils, and they blossom.

Scorpio Rabbit

Rabbits tend to be discreet people, and Scorpio Rabbits are the most tight-lipped of the lot. Scorpio Rabbits have a lot of secrets, and they enjoy keeping them. It gives them a wonderful feeling of superiority to think that they know things others don't. They have many secret ambitions too, and they don't like to speak of them in case others are pessimistic and pour scorn on their plans. So, it is the Scorpio Rabbit who is most likely to surprise everyone by suddenly reaching an amazing goal that no-one even knew he was aiming for.

Sagittarius Rabbit

Sporty Sagittarius brings a whole new dimension to the art-loving Rabbit. Rabbits are often indoor creatures, but Sagittarian Rabbits are much more adventurous in the open air than the usual bunny. They are sensuous and fun and attract many friends. They are also versatile and can turn their hands to several different careers if necessary. They like to get out and about more than most Rabbits and they are usually very successful.

Capricorn Rabbit

Capricorn Rabbits are great family folk. They firmly believe the family is the bedrock of life, and they work hard to keep their relations happy and together. The Capricorn Rabbit home is the centre of numerous clan gatherings throughout the year and weddings, birthdays, anniversaries and christenings are very important to them. Capricorn Rabbit will never forget the dates. These types are particularly interested in the past and will enjoy researching a family tree going back generations. If it ever crosses their minds that the rest of the tribe seems to leave all the donkey work to Capricorn Rabbit, he'd never say so. And, in truth, he doesn't really mind. There's nothing he loves more than having his family around him.

Aquarius Rabbit

The Aquarius Rabbit is a contradictory creature being both cautious and curious at the same time. These types crave security and love, and yet they have a great longing to find out more about everything around them. Fascinated by art, science and new inventions they love to potter about in book shops and tinker in the shed at home. Once they get an idea in their head, they can't rest until they have experimented with it, frequently forgetting to eat while they work. They need love and understanding.

Pisces Rabbit

The Pisces Rabbit is another bunny who needs a lot of understanding. Often gifted artistically they can sometimes be stubborn and awkward for no apparent reason. Yet when they are in the right frame of mind, they can charm the birds off the trees. It takes them a long time to make a friend, but when they do, it is a friend for life. The Pisces Rabbit home is full of beautiful things, and these subjects love to invite their most trusted friends to come and enjoy the magic.

CHAPTER 17: CREATE A WONDERFUL YEAR

By now, you should have a pretty good idea of the main zodiac influences on your lifestyle and personality, according to Chinese astrology. But how is 2024 going to shape up for you in general? Well, that largely depends on how cleverly you play your hand.

Dragon years are traditionally regarded as dynamic, prosperous and progressive. They are also fast moving. Changes abound in Dragon years. Every year brings its changes of course, but in Dragon years these tend to be more dramatic. Since the Dragon is regarded as a lucky sign most of the changes should be positive, but less positive upheavals can't be ruled out, particularly in the Autumn when the Dragon can turn sulky.

The key point is that – according to Chinese astrology – everything should be in balance. So, after the quieter energy that rippled just below the surface during last year's Year of the Rabbit, the world is now primed for a vitality boost. After 12 months of attempting to smooth things over and re-establish harmony – not always successfully – we're now poised for an optimistic leap of faith.

In 2024, the emphasis will be on innovation, creative risk-taking, entertainment in all its forms and scientific breakthroughs. A: 'Just Do it Now!' attitude will prevail.

Some signs will find these conditions more comfortable than others. Zodiac creatures that prefer to keep things as they are – those that tend to err on the side of caution and who like to reflect long and hard before committing themselves – could find 2024 a little unsettling. Energetic, always-on-the-go types, however, will rise to the challenges with joy. But, whichever group you belong to, as long as you're prepared – and you know what you might be up against – you can develop a strategy to ride those waves like a world-class surfer.

Sit back and rely on good fortune alone, because it's a terrific year for your sign, and you could snatch failure from the jaws of success. Navigate any stormy seas with skill and foresight if it's not such a sunny year for your sign, and you'll sail on to fulfil your dreams.

This is always true in any year, but doubly so when the dynamic Dragon is in charge. Be bold, brave and prepared to try, and the Dragon will smile on you. So, no matter what zodiac sign you were born under, the luck of the Dragon will help you… if you help yourself.

The future is not set in stone.

Chinese astrology is used very much like a weather forecast. You check out the likely conditions you'll encounter on your journey through the year, and plan your route and equipment accordingly. Some signs might need a parasol, sunscreen and sandals; while others require stout walking boots and rain gear.

Yet, properly prepared, both will end up in a good place at the end of the trip.

Finally, it's said that if you feel another sign has a much better outlook than you this year, you can carry a small symbol of that animal with you (in the form of a piece of jewellery, perhaps, or a tiny charm in your pocket or bag) and their good luck will rub off on you. Does it work? For some, maybe, but there's certainly no harm in trying.

Other Books from the Publisher

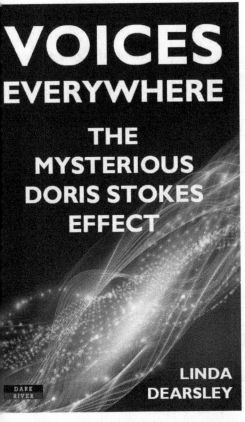

VOICES EVERYWHERE
THE MYSTERIOUS DORIS STOKES EFFECT

LINDA DEARSLEY

DARK RIVER

Linda Dearsley – *the author of this book* – was Doris Stokes' ghost.

Well, more accurately, she was the ghost-writer for Doris Stokes and worked with her for 10 years to produce 7 books, detailing the great lady's life.

In Voices Everywhere, Linda shines a light on her time working with Doris, right from the very early days when Doris was doing private readings in her Fulham flat, to filling the London Palladium and Barbican night after night, to subsequent fame outside the UK. Throughout all this, Doris Stokes never became anyone other than who she was: a kind, generous, and down-to-earth woman with an extraordinary gift, and a fondness for a nice p of tea. January 6th, 2020, would have been Doris' 100th birthday.

llowing Doris' death, Linda chronicles how cynics tried to torpedo the Stokes acy with accusations of cheating and dishonesty, but how those closest to Doris ver believed she was anything other than genuine.

turn, as the months and years rolled by, more and more intriguing people ossed Linda's path, each with their own unexplainable power, and Doris never emed far away. From the palmist who saw pictures in people's hands, to the uple whose marriage was predicted by Doris, and the woman who believes she ptures departed spirits on camera – the mysterious world of the paranormal, and oris Stokes' place within it, continues to unfold.

Karina Collins is acclaimed Tarot reader w
has helped people, from
walks of life, to bet
understand their liv
journeys.

Now, she is on a mission to h
you take control of your life
through the power of Tarot —
better explore a
understand your purpose a
destiny.

Do you have questions abc
now and your future? Perha
about making more money,
whether love is on the horizc
or whether you will becor
happier? Do you want to ste
your life in a direction th
brings success, pleasure, ar
fulfilment? Well, Tarot is
means to help you do exac
that! Used for centuries,
provides a powerful tool for unlocking knowledge, divining the future, ar
delivering shortcuts to the lives we desire.

In this full-colour top-rated book, Karina provides explanations and insights in
the full 78-card Tarot deck, how to phrase questions most effectively, real-wor
sample readings, why seemingly scary cards represent opportunities for grow
and triumph, and more.

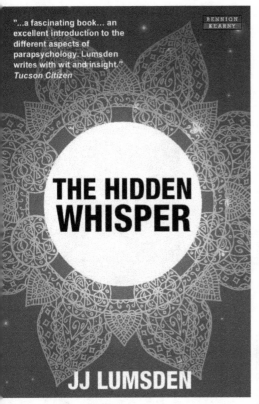

"...a fascinating book... an excellent introduction to the different aspects of parapsychology. Lumsden writes with wit and insight."
Tucson Citizen

A paranormal puzzle smoulders in the desert heat of southern Arizona. At the home of Jack and Chloe Monroe, a written message "Leave Now" appears then disappears, a candle in an empty room mysteriously lights itself, and – most enigmatically – an unidentifiable ethereal whisper begins to permeate the house. What was once simply strange now feels sinister. What once seemed a curiosity now seems terrifying.

Dr. Luke Jackson, a British Parapsychologist visiting family nearby, is asked to investigate and quickly finds himself drawn deeper into the series of unexplained events. Time is against him. He has just one week to understand and resolve the poltergeist case before he must depart Arizona.

The Hidden Whisper is the acclaimed paranormal thriller, written by real-life parapsychologist Dr. JJ Lumsden, which offers a rare opportunity to enter the intriguing world of parapsychology through the eyes of Luke Jackson. The fictional narrative is combined with extensive endnotes and references that cover Extra Sensory Perception, Psychokinesis, Haunts, Poltergeists, Out of Body Experiences, and more. If you thought parapsychology was like Ghostbusters – think again…

"This book works on many levels, an excellent introduction to the concepts current in the field of parapsychology… at best you may learn something new, and at worst you'll have read a witty and well-written paranormal detective story" Parascience.

A Practical Guide

MASTER YOUR CHRONIC PAIN

Dr Nicola Sherlock

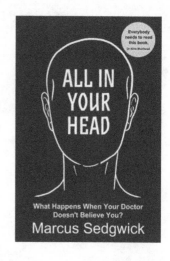

ALL IN YOUR HEAD

Everybody needs to read this book.
Dr Nina Sherlock

What Happens When Your Doctor Doesn't Believe You?
Marcus Sedgwick

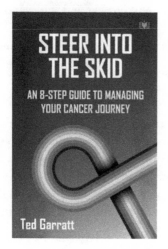

STEER INTO THE SKID

AN 8-STEP GUIDE TO MANAGING YOUR CANCER JOURNEY

Ted Garratt

Perform

& A sportsperson's guide to mental health and wellbeing

Thrive

Sarah Broadhead

Foreword by Jade Jones, OBE